THE 7 STAGES *of* SMALL-BUSINESS SUCCESS

THE 7 STAGES *of* SMALL-BUSINESS SUCCESS

From **STARTUP** *to*

SEVEN FIGURES

in **THREE YEARS**

OR LESS

CARL L. GOULD

KEYNOTE
PUBLISHING
A PART OF ADVANTAGE MEDIA GROUP

FEB 0 2 2011

Published by Keynote Publishing, Charleston, South Carolina.
Member of Advantage Media Group.

KEYNOTE PUBLISHING is a registered trademark and the Keynote colophon is a trademark of Advantage Media Group, Inc.

Printed in the United States of America.

ISBN: 978-1-59932-172-1
LCCN: 2009913785

This publication is designed to provide accurate and authoritative information in regard to the subject matter covered. It is sold with the understanding that the publisher is not engaged in rendering legal, accounting, or other professional services. If legal advice or other expert assistance is required, the services of a competent professional person should be sought.

Most Advantage Media Group titles are available at special quantity discounts for bulk purchases for sales promotions, premiums, fundraising, and educational use. Special versions or book excerpts can also be created to fit specific needs.

For more information, please write: Special Markets, Advantage Media Group, P.O. Box 272, Charleston, SC 29402 or call 1.866.775.1696.

Visit us online at **advantagefamily**.com

This book is dedicated to the entrepreneurial spirit, to those who dared to dream, and to those whose dreams have become our daily reality. This book is written for you in the hopes that I can in some small way repay the favor.

ACKNOWLEDGEMENTS

As in any project of this size and scope, there are more people who need to be acknowledged than space would permit. This book is more the cumulative work of countless contributors than just my efforts. I would first like to acknowledge the courage, bravery and passion of the thousands of entrepreneurs and business owners whom I have had the pleasure and privilege to coach over the years. I would like to thank Ann McIndoo for helping me get this idea out of my head and onto paper. To Denny Hocker and John Lawlor, who made sure that I structured the material in a way that made sense. Julia Nelson, thank you for making this book readable and "snarkier"! Kendra Granger for all of the graphics. The Advantage Media team for organizing these materials and getting this book into print. Yolanda Harris and her team at The Keynote Group for introducing me to all of the above.

An undertaking such as this would never happen without inspiration. Thank you Dr. Ichak Adizes for your brilliant work on Organizational Lifecycles and for your candid thoughts when you and I had the (all too) brief opportunity to connect and converse in the early 2000s. I continue to be inspired by the work of Harry S. Dent, researcher extraordinaire. Keith Harrell, you stirred me to think of my message in a totally new way, and for that I am grateful. Thank you, Eric Leaman for your guidance, consultation and friendship over the years as you helped me "hang up the hammer" and pursue my true life's work. Debbi Bifulco, who shows me what determination, courage and friendship looks like every time we meet. To my staff: Joann, Melissa and Brigitte, who are on the receiving end of "warp speed" dictation and yet somehow seem to capture every word. I thank you, I acknowledge you, and I appreciate you!

In the end, my ultimate motivation comes from my family. My wonderful wife, Chandra, and my three amazing children, Courtney, Sean and Vonya. They are a constant reminder to me that I am a blessed and lucky man. I work every day to make them as proud of me as I am of them.

TABLE OF CONTENTS

INTRODUCTION

This book is written as a result of my work with entrepreneurs, executives and business owners over the past two decades. I have coached and mentored the launch of more than 3,500 businesses, conducted more than 50,000 coaching sessions, and have interacted with hundreds of thousands of people who yearn to take their businesses (and their lives) to the next level. My assessment instruments have collected and analyzed millions of data points in the pursuit of answering one question, the most frequently asked question I get: "OK Carl, so I have this great idea, this personal breakthrough, NOW WHAT?" Many, if not most, business development models fall short of delivering that one simple answer. Most will give you some insight on what to do, or a clever way to repackage the same old information. Very few will show you HOW to do it. This book will address the HOW. I have observed the successful launch, growth and turnaround of businesses in more than 35 countries on six continents over the past two decades. There are clear patterns to success and failure. My observation is that all successful businesses go through 7 distinct stages, and I described them here.

This book is written for Business Owners/Entrepreneurs. BOE come in all shapes and sizes and yet are cut from the same mold of creativity, imagination, passion, strong will, and an insatiable appetite to make the world a better place as a result of their idea, product or service. The 7 Stages is written to give you a road map, or cookbook, for achieving that pinnacle.

This book is also written for all of the coaches, consultants, mentors and advisors who will guide BOE along the path of achieving their objective. While the recognizable face of every company tends to be its owner, the advisors are the ones who implement the brilliant ideas that BOE dream up. So, you "wizards behind the curtain," the 7 Stages is your tool to keep your BOE focused and on track.

Why I am writing this book? What you learn on these pages is the coaching and mentoring that I have been using with my clients for years. I have watched my clients embrace these methods and accelerate their results even beyond their own expectations. This book is my attempt to deconstruct my mentoring processes into a simple and easy-to-understand methodology. It is my hope to reach and impact on a global scale. Those with whom I have had the honor and pleasure to interact share one fundamental frustration: They want more from their business (and life), yet lack a road map to get there.

This book will help you identify where you are today in relation where you would ultimately like to be; create an action plan to get there; and keep you on track until you get there. Follow the steps, maximize the stages, and your vision will be realized. You cannot "out-dream" this methodology. It is as scaleable as your considerable imagination. As my golf instructor taught me, "Grip it high and let it fly!" This book will make sure you land on the fairway each time, and outdistance your mates!

A "Practical" Pep Talk

ONE OF THE GREAT LESSONS I have learned from observing BOEs around the world is that no goal is out of reach if you are fully committed to it, whatever the economic conditions. Economies move in cycles. You can't change or control the ups and downs in the market; what you can control is how you respond to them. Furthermore, opportunities present themselves in every economic climate.

At this writing, we are in one of the most severe market "corrections" (a nice way of saying that we are headed to hell in a hand basket!) that the world has ever seen. Real estate, stock markets, and other commodities are losing value on a daily basis. We are bombarded daily with negative predictions and the bottom is nowhere in sight.

On the face of it, this seems like bad news, but I contend that it depends on your point of view. If you find yourself unemployed and unprepared, or if your business is suffering greatly, then this stage of the economic cycle certainly is bad news. But what if you had prepared your business to produce multiple streams of income? What if you had a strategy to generate revenue in a growing economy, a shrinking economy, and a fluctuating market environment? No one thinks it's foolish to own a parka, a bathing suit and an umbrella, even though you know you'll probably never need all of them at once. If you need clothes for every kind of weather, doesn't it make just as much sense to have a strategy for any economic climate?

My good friend Steve Linder, a stock-trading expert, often says, "You can't predict the markets, but you can anticipate them." This maxim also applies to running a successful business. Anticipate the ups and downs of the marketplace and have a product, service or offering that is appropriate for each circumstance.

An upward trending marketplace is full of excitement and enthusiasm. People are looking for the next big thing or the next hot commodity. Formulate a strategy that takes advantage of the momentum: Run with the bulls! An example of an up-market strategy is up-selling your customers. Whatever your product or service, have upgrades or premium versions available. If you are selling new cars or new homes, people will be more apt to opt for the granite countertops or the leather seats. Offer extra perks with your services for a modest fee increase. Credit is usually easy to come by in an up market, so make sure you give your customer something to buy with it!

A downward-trending market is characterized by fear and angst. Panic can set in as consumers hunker down as if a storm were brewing. Walmart has carefully studied its consumers' buying patterns over the years. It is famous for stocking up locales with particular commodities, such as strawberry Pop-tarts, before hurricanes and tropical storms. By anticipating what customers want, it is able to sell out entire shipments of goods. You can use the same tactic to learn what your customers want during particular market conditions, and provide it to them quickly and conveniently.

Consumers in a down market will look for a way to get the most for their money. They want products and services that will meet a variety of their needs without costing extra. "Bundling" — adding products or services to a purchase at no extra charge — is a great strategy for the

BOE to utilize. Down-market consumers want to hoard, not indulge: You can feed that appetite by bundling ancillary products and services to their purchases. If you have watched a bird build a nest, you will notice that it gathers a variety of materials. Often it will use coarse twigs for the outer part, and line the inside with something finer and softer. Your product can be like that nest: a bundle of various items or services that combine to make the customer feel taken care of. Your customers will appreciate the added value.

A sideways-trending market is characterized by uncertainty. Will it go up or down? The experts are always divided. Most consumers in a flat market will adopt a "wait and see" attitude with their purchases. They are looking for security and predictability. This can express itself in the tendency to purchase membership in a club, group, or organization that gives consumers a sense of community and enhances their lifestyles. This makes subscription services a great sideways strategy. Rather than charge for your product or service, you can give it to customers for "free" or at a deep discount once they have signed up for a level of ongoing services (often referred to as a continuity agreement). Subscriptions services can be priced at varying levels (such as Bronze, Silver and Gold) to appeal to a variety of demographic categories. Remember that in a flat market, customers will hold out for a great deal; make sure the perceived value of what you are offering is greater than the fee you are charging.

Noah built the ark *before* the rains fell. Talk about a great down-market strategy! Arm yourself ahead of time with strategies for up, down and flat market conditions and you will be ready to profit no matter what happens. I advise my clients to have at least five streams of income for their businesses, with at least one stream set up to thrive in each of the three major market conditions. A 2008 survey of the companies that we advise worldwide revealed that nearly two out of three outperformed their economic conditions[1] and more than a third had their best year ever in 2008.

We are faced with unprecedented economic turbulence, and yet such times present unique opportunities. They demand that BOEs focus on their objectives and utilize all their creativity, faith and willpower to see them through. History has shown that *someone* will be able to embrace chaotic market conditions and apply the appropriate strategies, profiting tremendously. If you develop and implement your strategies wisely, your business can thrive in any economic climate. Remember, it's not the economy; it is how you respond to it. May your business achieve its full potential so that you can enjoy the fruit of your labor and live life on your own terms!

---

1 The National Bureau of Economic Research (http://www.nber.org/cycles/dec2008.html) tracks the 'beginning and ending dates of U.S. recessions"…and that "The committee determined that the decline in economic activity in 2008 met the standard for a recession". According to RECESSION.ORG (http://recession.org/definition), "…a true economic recession can only be confirmed if GDP (Gross Domestic Product) growth is negative for a period of two or more consecutive quarters." "The year to date performance of major equity indices (i.e. stock markets)…[demonstrated]…a decline of 36% year to date" according to Seeking Alpha (http://seekingalph.com/article/105113-year-to-date-stock-market-performance-by-country). While U.S. statistics were the benchmark for our survey, the "economic conditions" I refer to above denote the overall economic downturn worldwide. According to the Seeking Alpha market-advice Web site, 81 of 84 countries highlighted in its research of national stock market performance showed a decline in P/E ratios of an average of 40%. Further, "Economy Review '12/23/2008 2008 in Review: Mortgage Crisis Forever Changes Wall Street'" commented "Over the last 12 months that were ruled by negative economic indicators and widespread fear, the S&P Index decreased about 40 percent, for a loss of more than $6 trillion." My research shows that for all practical purposes, "economic conditions" deteriorated 40% globally in 2008. Our survey of 767 companies that a CMT Mentor advises showed that two thirds outperformed these economic conditions and one third had their best year ever in the history of their company in 2008. This affirms our contention that the 7 Stage Process is a road map to success for an entrepreneurial business, regardless of economic conditions.

CHAPTER 1:

DEFINING THE GAME AND THE GALAXY YOU'LL PLAY IN

For centuries, almost everyone assumed that bigger was better. Bigger cars, bigger hair and bigger companies were all signs that you had made it. Corporations swelled to the point that no one could possibly keep track of what was going on. Somewhere along the line, we learned the benefits of specialization. Now, small is the new big: fuel-efficient cars, ultra-thin notebook computers, and tiny cell phones. In the 21st century, small businesses are the new big businesses.

This book is for all those small-business owners, a term I'll define in more detail below. Interestingly, businesses of all sizes actually have a lot in common. You'll notice that people come in all shapes and sizes, but also share some common qualities. The path to success and fulfillment in life goes through several stages. Age doesn't determine success; aligning your actions with your core values does. You serve yourself and those around you best when you live a life congruent with your values and on your own terms.

Successful businesses are much the same: They may look completely different on the outside, but each of them progresses through seven simple stages of development as they realize the vision of the owner. The more an entrepreneur understands and embraces these seven stages, the better his or her chance of creating a business that will thrive during each stage and endure for the long haul. Amazingly, when you learn to manage these seven simple stages, you can take your business from startup to seven figures in three years or less.

We tend to think of a business as the building that houses a particular industry or even the tax-identification status of an organization. For the purposes of this book, think about your business primarily as a system for economic exchange. This exchange covers the transfer of anything of value between you and another party. You could be selling software or lawn care; your business provides the mechanism that allows that exchange to happen.

My purpose is to help the owners of small and medium-size businesses (companies with fewer than 250 employees), as well the heads of the divisions of larger companies. Learning about the 7 Stages will allow these leaders to develop their organizations so they can stop doing everything themselves. Only then can they begin to fulfill the dream that started their businesses in the first place.

READY FOR A VACATION?

An easy way to determine the degree to which you are directly involved in your business' day-to-day activities is to ask yourself how much time you can take off. If everything will collapse if you go to the beach for the weekend, your systems (your business) are underdeveloped, to say the least. If you can go to Europe for a month and come home to find everything running as well as if you were there (or better!) your business is in much better shape.

My goal for small-business owners is not just to make their organizations financially successful, but also to help them enjoy the process. Every business mirrors the personality, strengths and blind spots of its owner or leader. If the owner is friendly and gregarious but lacks organizational skills, the company will probably have great customer service but weak follow-up. An owner who is driven and decisive but insensitive may find that his company finishes every order on time but has difficulty keeping customers. He or she may even alienate the internal customer: the employees. This phenomenon means that a little introspection on the owner's part can do wonders to improve the entire organization.

VOCABULARY LESSON

Let's clarify a few popular terms before we go any further.

Sole proprietors are just what that sounds like: a one-man (or -woman) show. Many sole proprietors aspire to build an organization, but may feel constrained by time or finances. The sole proprietor can still apply the principles of the 7ß Stages to develop his processes and eventually build a team to leverage various tasks.

A **micro-business** has one to 10 employees. If you're working with yourself and a few others, you've got a micro-business. In these kinds of organizations, everyone has to wear a lot of different hats. They end up servicing the business and client at the same time: They answer phones, fill orders, develop advertising campaigns, and make the coffee. A large percentage of all businesses are actually micro-businesses. In fact, 95.5% of all businesses have 20 or fewer employees.

A **small business** has between 11 and 50 employees. If you have a small business, you can't manage every employee personally, but you probably know them all. You may have a couple of different departments and you might have a corporate structure of sorts. In a small business, even with different departments and divisions you can have your hand in just about anything – and you probably do. You can help solve a lot of problems this way, but you can create plenty too!

The **medium-size business** has between 51 and 250 employees. Generally, if you have fewer than 150 employees in one locale, everyone still gets a chance to know one another. They'll naturally spend time hanging out in the break room, near the water cooler, or in the cafeteria. Everyone's face will be familiar. Between 150-250 employees, the dynamics change a little bit. That number is too large to expect a sense of camaraderie to develop across the group. You will need to create multiple divisions in order to foster effective teamwork.

For this reason, many of the largest multinational corporations will not allow any division of their company get larger than 150 employees. They'll erect a building and put 150 parking spaces in the parking lot. When that parking lot is filled, they will put up a new building. If you take your medium-size business to 250 employees, you will find that structure is vital and systems are absolutely indispensable.

By the way, the term "small business" is often used as a catch-all to include the sole proprietor along with micro, small and medium businesses. I took the time to define them in greater detail so that each entrepreneur can have a better sense of his or her starting point on the Success Cycle™.

Finally, let's define **big business**. A big business is a company with 251 employees or more. You can have 251 employees or you can have

50,000 employees; no matter how "big" it is, is a collection of small businesses or divisions.

We will talk at length about a business model called **The Galaxy Model™**. This is the most efficient way to build an organization of any size. To learn more, go to www.the-7stages.com/galaxy to learn the steps of building a Galaxy Organization. This will show you how to grow such an organization and take your current one to the next level. You want to build a Galaxy organization, whether you are micro, small, medium or big business.

In The Galaxy Model, you will have one central technology: your brand name or trademark. A number of independent divisions revolve around this central technology just like planets around the sun. These are the departments or functions of the company, which are all aligned with its mission, vision, values and purpose. Each division is synchronized with every other division, all serving the customer and serving one another. That's The Galaxy Model in a nutshell.

MEET THE BOE: YOU!

Now, who runs all this? (Hint: It's probably the person reading these words.) If you are the one launching a new business, expanding an existing enterprise, or turning one around, you've already got a nickname. You are the **BOE: the business owner-entrepreneur.**

Whether you are a man or woman, old or young, from any culture, race or creed, there are many things all BOEs have in common. You're both an artist and a technician. You're probably brilliant at what you do and tend to see things bigger and better than they are. You're a visionary and dreamer, and you find working for someone else confining.

If you're starting a business, it's most likely because all the jobs you've held or businesses you've run in the past didn't fulfill your vision. You see something new that has been created, or hasn't been realized in its fullest form. That is what drives you.

BOEs are forward-thinking. They are always excited about something new. They like variety and often get bored easily. (Sound familiar?) They don't believe in problems, so they call them challenges. Often, when they overcome one challenge they're off to tackle a new one.

BOEs prefer innovation to living in the past. Rather than jazz up a product that isn't selling, why not create a new product? The BOE is always trying to fix the old by introducing something new. This is probably not your first entrepreneurial venture, nor will it be your last. I want to make sure it's successful, wherever it falls in your list of achievements.

PLANNING, PLANNING, PLANNING

Now, for everyone's favorite part: the spreadsheets, the structure and the systems. Yes, it's time for the glamorous and sexy world of planning.

While those particular activities might not light your fire, the results they produce will. In the rest of the book, I will detail planning methods and strategies that will enable your business to become efficient, effective and successful. Spreadsheets might be dull, but their results will help you realize your vision.

When you really consider why you got into business in the first place, it probably had very little to do with money. As a matter of fact, money ranks startlingly low on the list when entrepreneurs are asked why they started their businesses. For most BOEs, money is not the goal; it is a means to an end. Your vision for the company doesn't involve mountains of debt and poorly paid employees, so you're going to need to financially profitable.

The step-by-step systematic process of The 7 Stages will help you earn what you deserve. It will do this not by helping you demand a better salary, but by causing you to exchange so much value with your customers and clients that they will *ask* to give you money.

If that sounds like a plan you can get excited about, read on!

CHAPTER 2

THE DISCOVERY PROCESS

So what is this "business DISCoverY" process? In short, it's a system that I developed not only to help you understand your business better, but to discover the personality of your business. It is a journey of self-discovery because the personality of a business will mirror that of its owner. Your individual strengths will become the strengths of the business and your blind spots will become the blind spots of the business, which means it is vital to learn what drives you and what slows you down.

You'll notice the unique way we write "DISCoverY." In the 1920s and '30s, Dr. William Moulton Marston developed a theory called DISC, where the initials D, I, S and C represented the four major categories of personalities. For our purposes, they represent the four sections (and types of personnel) of your business. The "Y" is the "why" of your business: why you do what you do. Another way it reads is "DISC" over "Y", or Behaviors over Values.

Values, in a practical sense, are your priorities. What is most important to you in your life right now? What gets you up early in the morning and keeps you up late at night? What activities, no matter how demanding, energize you and put a smile on your face? The DISCoverY process shows you *how* you do things (your personal style), *why* you do things (your priorities based on what is most important and urgent to you in your life), as well as your *attributes* (your personal skills and talents).

At the end of the day, you will exert an extraordinary amount of your energy on the business, far more than anyone else. That is why the personality of your business will reflect your own. The goal of discovering those qualities is not to make value judgments about whether you are good or bad, smart or stupid. Quite simply, it's better to know from the beginning where your strengths and growth areas are. That enables you to build on your strengths and take advantage of help or expertise regarding your blind spots.

STRENGTHS AND BLIND SPOTS

When you're driving, your blind spot is the portion of your view obstructed by the frame of your car. It's not your fault you can't see it: You just need to know where it is so you can check it when you're making a lane change. In life, we all have blind spots as well. Some husbands make plenty of money, but have to rely on their wives to balance the checkbook. A software engineer may write brilliant code, but struggle to explain how it works to someone outside the industry. Blind spots don't indicate a lack of skill or intelligence, just varying areas of focus. You're "blind" to that particular area because you don't spend much time looking at it.

We all gravitate toward certain activities and away from others, based on our proficiency and enjoyment. Activities that attract us become strengths, while those we neglect, intentionally or unintentionally, become blind spots. With focus and effort, you can turn any blind spot into a strength.

The DISCoverY process helps you to become very aware of your strengths and conscious of your blind spots. Your goal is to understand what strengths are required to make your business successful and then do what you do best. Then you can delegate the rest to those with strengths in those particular areas. However, you will not know what to delegate if you are not aware of your blind spots.

There is no one person who possesses every quality and skill needed to run a successful business. Yet you need have it all. You need strong direction, big-picture planning, and a strong vision that drives the company. You must have robust sales, strong income, and interaction with your market. You need a structured and systematic approach to everything: consistent systems with plenty of quality controls.

Furthermore, any successful business works constantly to improve quality. In the DISCoverY process we call this constant improvement I^3Q (pronounced "eye-cubed"), which stands for Intelligent, Incremental Improvements to Quality™. The business that utilizes I^3Q works smarter, not harder, and focuses on achievement rather than on activity. "Busy" used to mean "successful" in the business world. "We're very busy" meant "we're doing very well." In today's world, being busy may be a sign that you are not optimizing your time and your resources.

Discovering your strengths and blind spots will allow you all the time that you need to create a balance between your business and your life. This means you have the time to harvest and enjoy the fruit of your efforts and take care of your business well. Your business doesn't have to own and consume you. We do recognize that you are an entrepreneur and you will work a great deal anyway. However, your business will be healthier in the long term when you are a healthier, balanced individual. Knowing what to do yourself and what to delegate is key to striking this balance.

WHAT EVERY SUCCESSFUL BUSINESS NEEDS

Every business is different, but there are some things we can say confidently that every successful business needs:

- *Money.* Remember what we said about robust sales and income. Business is a game of cash. If you're not bringing it in, you're not in the game.

- *Significant customer experience.* Your interaction with your marketplace is very important too; you need to give all your customers a memorable experience when they purchase your product or service.

- *Strong systems.* Systems need to be structured, consistent, reliable, efficient and effective. They also need to create a growing relationship with your clients and market that delivers certainty. No one person can be all things to all people. As far as your widget is concerned, your company must be all things to its customers, or you risk losing those customers to your competition. A study on customer satisfaction and loyalty shows that 40% of happy and satisfied customers reported that they would leave and purchase from the competition even though they were happy and satisfied with the original company.[2]

- *Strong controls.* The details of your business must be handled with excellence.

- *High quality.* The quality of the agreement you have with your vendors, the product, and your service must be high and ever-increasing. Unless you have found a way to corner the

---

2 Source: Shep Hyken: *Moments of Magic.*

market on oxygen, your product or service is a commodity, not a necessity. The relationship and experience that you create for your customers is priceless. You must constantly improve quality or you'll be passed by.

As you work to create deeper relationships with your customers, you will deliver a significant experience that they find enjoyable. That is what triggers activity from your customers and will keep them coming back.

THE FOUR PERSONALITY TYPES

Once you've determined your business needs and identified those strengths and blind spots, you're going to decide how to appropriately allocate your energy and resources. To take an assessment to identify your strengths and blind spots, please go to www.the7stages.com. In each of the 7 Stages, you will have a major focus and minor focus. You'll give one particular area a great deal of time and effort without ignoring everything else. You'll notice that each stage will have distinct characteristics as the business continues to absorb your personality. Remember, it's *your* flexibility, drive, vision and passion that will get the business off the ground. You're going to need every bit of it!

Once you're soaring, however, that same impulsiveness and spontaneity can crash the plane or (worse yet!) take you to the wrong destination. Be sure to maximize your flexibility in the beginning with the minimal controls; once you're in the air, it's time to follow the flight plan. You can even go on autopilot.

Now, let's turn our attention to the other people in your business. *DISC – The Universal Language*, by Bill J. Bonnstetter and Judy Suiter, outlines the four basic types of people. First, there are very **dominant** personalities. These are the doers; they're demanding, directive, decisive. They get things done. They want results.

Second, you have the **influencers**. These are enthusiastic and optimistic. They are inspiring, effusive, gregarious, outgoing, and they love to have fun.

The third type of person is very **supportive** and needs structure and security a great deal. They make great supporting players: They're very sincere, stable, steady and consistent. They enjoy a slower pace, working as team, and building consensus.

The fourth kind of people are the **compliant** ones: They follow all the rules and insist on doing everything by the book. These are the detail-oriented people who love to analyze everything. They like charts, graphs, and being right all the time. (Or as I was lectured once by a Compliant, "We don't like to be right, we like to be correct.") These are your perfectionists.

Fortunately, these four types of people correlate with the four basic functions of a company: D, I, S, and C. D is the dominant personality and the **direction** of your business. This is the big-picture planning, the mission, vision, values and purpose. Your direction answers the questions: Where are we going? Where will we be in five years? What is important to us? Why do we exist?

I is not only your influencer, but also the **interaction** and **income** of your business. The income is literally everything that *comes into* the business: your sales, your interactions, marketing responses, and your customer service. All these involve something coming in or interacting with someone.

The S is your steady **supporter** and it's also your systems. These are all the day-to-day activities that keep your business running and prevent it from falling apart. There are two types of systems: "Yes" Systems and "No" Systems. A "No" System is a process that is necessary whether or not a customer places and order. "No" Systems include activities such as getting the mail, answering the phone, turning on the lights, and locking up at the end of the day. It means responsibilities such as who sorts the mail, sends out the invoices and files the receipts. Then there are the systems and operations that fulfill the customer order when it comes in. That is a "Yes" System. "Yes" Systems are the steps you take to fulfill a customer order.

"YES" SYSTEMS AND "NO" SYSTEMS IF YOU WERE A HOTEL...

'No' Systems would mean that you had no reservations for that evening. What would still have to be in place? You would have to staff the building, have clean linens on the beds, fill the kitchen with food, have the daily newspaper, have an operator standing by, etc. "No" Systems are constant, "Yes" Systems are variable based on the number of customer orders.

"Yes" Systems would be all of the activities needed when a customer contacts the hotel and wants to become a guest. What would you need in order to satisfy that request? A system for booking the reservations, checking in the guests, bringing the luggage to the sleeping rooms, cleaning the rooms, parking the cars, lifeguarding the pool, readying the shuttles, etc.

The C is your compliant individual and the **controls** in your business. Your controls are all the details that ensure you get things right the first time. This includes the wording of your contracts and (later) all of your policies and procedures manuals. How low do you turn the air conditioning in the summer? We don't want to spend too much money, but we don't want the computers to fry.

Don't underestimate the importance of all these details and nuances in giving you a competitive advantage. You might be making a lot of money (that's I, or income), but it's up to the C (control) to make sure you keep it. As the old saying goes, it's not what you make, it's what you keep. I can guarantee someone with a very high C component in his or her personality came up with that.

YOUR PERSONALITY STYLE

These four personality styles are nothing new. The ancient Greek doctor Hippocrates taught about the Four Humors, from which modern psychology derived the Four Temperaments. The choleric would correspond to D, sanguine to I, phlegmatic to S, and melancholic to C.

You actually possess all four of these elements in your personality: Part of you is dominant, part is an influencer, part of you is a supporter, and part a compliant. Your natural style is determined by the degree to which your personality emphasizes those different aspects.

All of us are "wired" a certain way: our natural style. You also have an adapted style. That is your response to your environment: what you think you *should* be and attempt to become. Your natural style might be very steady and slower-paced. If you get a job in an emergency room, it might require you to become very spontaneous and to move at a fast pace. Your style then adapts to the demands of your job.

In the typical company, some salesmen may feel they don't fit the traditional salesman style: loud, fast-talking and animated. They may adapt to this image without realizing they can be successful in their natural style. We tend to adapt our behavior based on our perception of our environment or in direct response to the environment. This can be helpful, but it can also lead to frustration.

The DISCoverY process will help ensure that you build your business around your true style, not your adaptive one. This means that you enter an industry and build an organization that agrees with who you naturally are. That will set you up for long- term success in your business and in life.

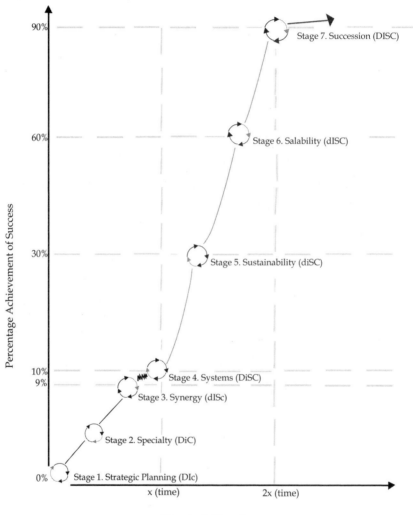

90% — Stage 7. Succession (DISC)

60% — Stage 6. Salability (dISC)

Percentage Achievement of Success

30% — Stage 5. Sustainability (diSC)

10% — Stage 4. Systems (DiSC)
9% — Stage 3. Synergy (dISc)

Stage 2. Specialty (DiC)

0% — Stage 1. Strategic Planning (DIc)

x (time)   2x (time)

Time to Achieve Success

CHAPTER 3

THE SUCCESS CYCLE: AN OVERVIEW

T he success cycle is an achievement-focused methodology for how to achieve your desired objectives with the least resistance and in the most effective and efficient manner. Much has been written about the life cycles of a corporation, business, an animal, a region, a person. We all know people who never got the most out of life. We all know businesses that never really thrived. Our focus here is on success. We have taken the best of what makes a business successful. And we have managed that success cycle.

When aligning your short-term effectiveness with long-term efficiency (meaning your day-to-day activities aligned with the overall vision of your company), you have the best opportunity to go from start-up to seven figures in three years or less. By following that success cycle, you have duration of approximately 36 months. The start-up or early stages of the cycle would be Stages 1-3. You'll move into Stage 4, and then go from there onward in the second 18 months. Stage 4 is the fulcrum, the pivot point.

In the Success Cycle™, you're going to focus on the activities that will produce the greatest result at any given time. This is an achievement-focused methodology. It's step-by-step, structured and systematic. It will produce significant results and you'll have fun doing it as well. Very enjoyable.

When you have the proper structure in place and you have the proper systems behind it, that releases the energy of the business. It empowers your employees and enables them to create a significant, consistent and very predictable experience for your customers. When you do that, when you take the certainty of a consistent system and its high quality, a very significant experience for the customer, you create a connection with your customers that takes your business and their experience to a higher level. As a result, your business will stand out as a leader in that particular field and your results will be accelerated.

Within the Success Cycle, you're going to channel your energy toward the result in a very achievement-focused way 90% of the time. Ten percent of your time will be spent identifying the challenge and opportunity at hand. You will spend 90% of your energy focusing on achieving that solution. When you put your major focus on the outcome, solution and result, you will move through the Success Cycle in a very quick manner.

We can draw from other patterns of success for your business. I'll just talk about the most recent era of commerce. The current dynamic is: The time it takes a product to reach 10% market penetration is the same time it takes that business to achieve the remaining 90% success.

For automobiles, mobile phones and record albums (if you remember those), DVDs, television sets, VCRs, it took the same amount of time for 10% of the population to own one as it did for the remaining 90% of the population to own one. That has been consistent throughout business and commerce.

It's the same for the Success Cycle. It takes approximately 18 months for a business to go from start-up to Stage 3 on the cusp of Stage 4. Then, it takes approximately another 18 months for that business to go from Stage 4 to 7, which would be a seven-figure business producing consistent cash flow with a team in place that you could then sell, will or pass on to another generation, for you to create a legacy company.

It may not even be your goal to go through all seven stages. The Success Cycle is designed to help you maximize each stage. And, then, if you choose, you can move to the next stage.

You may be asking yourself, "Why wouldn't I want to have a goal of being a seven-stage business or getting through the succession stage?" Well, you could be a musical performer, a singer, an actor or brain surgeon. You very much like doing what you do. By definition, that means you will stay at probably Stage 2 or 3, maybe a Stage 4 business.

If you take a musical act like the Rolling Stones, they're a Stage 2/3 business. They will be there forever, because you can't delegate out Mick Jagger. Mick has to sing the songs. People come to see Mick. If the Rolling Stones were going on tour, but four or five other guys were going to play their music, they wouldn't draw nearly as many people to the stadiums. They probably wouldn't have much of a tour at all.

If you go to a doctor for brain surgery and that doctor says to you, "Well, I'm not the one that's going to do the cutting, surgery; I'm just here to meet with you now and going to send somebody else in," you might lose your confidence in that particular procedure. You want your brain surgeon. You want to go see your Rolling Stones. You want to see your performer.

You don't have to go to Stage 7 to be as successful. You maximize the stage you're in and you can stay there forever, or you can move on. It's your choice.

Keep in mind that throughout the course of the success cycle, any frustration you have in your business is because you lack an effective structure or an efficient system in your business. The moment you put in an effective structure and efficient system, you will again release that energy and have more energy to give to your clients and to create the work-life balance sought by starting this business in the first place.

NYU STUDY

What drives a business up and down the success cycle? A 1978 New York University Sloan School of Business study of 3,500 businesses found a 95% correlation between the value of the business and its balance sheets (meaning the numbers). The numbers on the balance sheets correlated 95% with the overall value of that business.

Let's fast-forward to the new millennium. According to the follow up of the same study in 2004, there is now a 28% correlation between the numbers on a business' balance sheet and the value of the business. What has changed? Where is the other 72%? What is the 72% that drives performance and value of that business? In the new millennium, that would be the people and their performance.

Let's talk about another study, by Cornell University. The major finding was that up to one-third of employees are in the wrong job. Another third were wrong for the business and their culture. Up to one half of the people in the business are not prepared for the future of their business. That is staggering. What does it say? If they're in the wrong job, not aligned with the culture, and not prepared for the future, there is no alignment in this company, or very little.

If you have this much *mis*alignment, you have very little lift. When 72% of what drives the value of a company is the people and their performance, this is a crisis. If you are an established business, you are probably experiencing the consequence of these two studies right now. It's time for you to identify where you are on the success cycle, because it's never too late to turn it around. We are focused on success, on your achieving your result. We identify where you are right now, where you want to go, and how you're going to get there.

There are certain activities that you will take on, but you don't always have to be active to be achieving. Sometimes, there will be addition by subtraction, meaning, there are certain things you will never do again. You might reduce your activity in certain areas, thereby raising the level of achievement in your business.

DEVELOPING THE TALENT IN YOUR ORGANIZATION

We've identified the challenges, the problems that you face when you're not aligned, and where you might be on that success cycle and how you want to bring yourself forward in that success cycle. What happens if you do? What happens when you take this methodology and put it into place and you align the people and maximize their performance? Here is what can happen.

The aforementioned Cornell study shows that if you do align the people in your organization, you have the potential for a 15%-20% greater survival rate of that business. And the market value of that business can rise by up to $40,000 or more per employee.

Let's go back to what we can do or what this methodology can do in order to drive the 72% performance of a company. Working with a strategic partner (a coach, mentor, consultant, advisor), having the awareness of your strengths, knowing who is right for the business and putting those people in place, you can raise the productivity of your employees, and therefore the company, by up to 800%. On average, this type of work has shown to return $8 of productivity for every dollar spent in nurturing, growing and developing the talent of your organization. That's what you're doing: You're developing the talent in your organization.

DREAMS REQUIRE HARD WORK

In the success cycle, you have chosen to make a great leap of faith,. You are now the business owner. I heard someone say recently, "Well, it was my dream to be a business owner." I asked this person: "Are you living the dream or is it a nightmare?" And he said, "Well, I really thought I was going to make more money, get more time." I asked: "You have kids, right?" "Yes, I do." "Did you have children because you wanted more sleep?" He thought about it for a moment and realized what he had gotten himself into by starting a business.

We all have a dream that starting and owning a business is our path to freedom, and it is. It absolutely is. On your way to heaven, you must dip your toes and walk through the path of hell on your way there. Success in business can be elusive, because it's hard. But, as Tom Hanks said in *A League of Their Own*, one of my favorite movies, "The hard is what makes it great. If it were easy, everyone would be doing it."

Keep in mind your business needs to be nurtured, just as you would nurture a pet, a baby. For this dream to remain a dream, for you to achieve your vision, you have to have the right people in the right job align with the company mission, vision, values and purpose. There is no other way.

We are all going to define our success differently. What is it to you? More time, money? Did you build this business to get more acclaim, acknowledgement and status? Is it for family reasons? Did you want to create a legacy? Did you want to contribute something to society? Did you want to make a contribution to a church or charity? We all have our own reasons for going into business, dreaming. As we've said, by focusing on achievement over activity, by working smarter rather than harder, we can go very systematically through the seven stages or we can maximize the stage where we are in order to realize our dream.

SPREADSHEETS, PLANNING, WEEKLY MEETINGS

How do you go from start-up to seven figures in just three years? That might seem like an incredibly daunting task. But it's really not. It is about synchronizing and aligning your activity, very effective day-to-day activity, and short-term effectiveness with your long-term efficiency. That efficiency will be determined by how aligned you are with your big-picture planning. Keep it very simple, structured and systematic.

Spreadsheets, planning and weekly meetings will become some of the sexiest things you'll ever do in business. When I first heard that, I thought, "Maybe I should rethink being in a business. This is not what I want for my life." Now, I can't wait for these things. It's not necessarily the spreadsheet, whether I'm producing or reading it, that's sexy, that satisfies me; it's the result I get from it. Because I'm organized, structured and I have systems, I reap the benefits of the results. That's what we're after.

It has been said that being a business owner is the toughest and loneliest position in business. Do you know what makes it tough and lonely? You're flying by the seat of your pants in the middle of the night with no gauges or flight plan. To make it easier, simpler and more enjoyable, simply plan things out in the stages. Don't skip a stage. Take them step by step by step. And enjoy each step as you go. It's a wonderful, rewarding evolution of yourself, the people in your business, your customers, and the business itself.

THE 7 STAGES: AN OVERVIEW

What are these 7 Stages? We've been talking about them a lot. Let me give you an overview of each stage before we get more into it.

Stage 1 is the Strategic Planning stage. This is where your dream is born. You're going to focus on the direction, the planning of your company. You're going to sell your business first. Then, you're going to create it. What the heck does that mean?

Have you ever heard of a franchise? McDonald's founder Ray Kroc, way back when, had the idea of selling businesses to people when they didn't exist and then creating them later on. He actually had to convince the government that it was not fraudulent. Have you ever bought a home or apartment just by looking at the building plans when there was nothing but a hole in the ground? That builder and developer sold the business first, created it second.

A very common practice when sports arenas are built today is to sell what is called personal seat licenses. Before construction is completed, owners sell the right to buy a seat once it's made. In other words, they sell out the whole stadium before it exists.

Have you ever bought a ticket to a performance that has not debuted yet? Have you ever prepurchased a book, DVD or CD before it was released? Anyone who presells something is selling the business first and creating it second.

If your goal is to have at least one paying customer, then you have the minimum goal of getting to Stage 2. Remember, I'm not here to tell you what stage is the right one for you. Unless you're in this for exercise, you will automatically go to Stage 2 the moment anyone purchases your product, service or idea (widget). If your goal is to have one paying customer, that means your goal is to get to at least Stage 2. You can stay at any stage forever.

As soon as someone pays you, though, you will leave Stage 1. You can maximize Stage 1 by doing your planning. Once that is done, you have your first client and move to Stage 2, the specialty stage. Since you have a paying client, you now have a job to do. You focus on continuously implementing your direction, pushing through. The marketplace will resist, but you must push through. And you also want to build the quality of your product and service. Build your credentials. And, you can have a minor focus on sales. You need to keep that cash coming in early on, especially. So, you want the quality to go up and to build your core competency, and you can stay here forever. Your clients will love you and they will keep coming back.

Every stage, by the way, is divided into trimesters: an early, mid and late part. I bring that up here because Stage 2 is where most businesses reside. The Rolling Stones are in late Stage 2, very mature part of the stage. In the early part of the stage, you're going to focus on the quality of your product. If you've just launched a pizzeria or a deli, you need to make sure you have the best food so word gets around and people come back. How much you might discount or charge is less important than making a high-quality product.

Then, as you move into the mid part of the stage, you want to build your brand, credentials. Gather testimonials and case studies. Continue to hone the quality of your product, skills, education and credentials. As you move into late Stage 2, you want to be an expert in your field. You want to be among the highest-paid and have the highest acclaim or credentials in your particular field. You want to be known as the master in that particular area.

Stage 3 is the Synergy Stage: And a Sandbox Is Born. You know you're in Stage 3 when you've just hired somebody else. Why is a sandbox born? You need to play nice with others in the sandbox. No throwing or kicking sand, biting, punching, scratching. You're going to focus on delegating, building that structure that we talked about, that organizational chart. You're going to train other people and delegate control. You need to be patient with yourself here. Very important. The reason you need to be patient is quality might dip just a bit, because you've leveraged some of your tasks and you've trusted and delegated those tasks and results to other people. They might not do it as well as you. You need to manage yourself. You are your toughest client.

And Stage 3 is the graveyard for most businesses; it is where most will fail and is the toughest 1% of growth in your business. If you have that growth, you have made it through the "Miracle 1%". You are among the minority of businesses that will ever make it out of this stage. Only one out of 10 businesses will be ultimately successful. You will be that one, because you've made it through the Miracle 1%.

Stage 3 is a graveyard for small-business owners because it requires you to not only manage yourself, but also to start putting structure in place.

This is the same structure that you moved away from earlier in your career *or* neglected in your last business or enterprise.

Hear what I'm saying now: There are no systems yet. We do not want systems that will stifle the initial launch or turnaround of the business. It's too early. What we want is *structure* (a team around you), and you need to be flexible. You need to place trust in others even when you see them making mistakes. This is hard for entrepreneur, especially when one is so technically savvy in the business. Self-management becomes very important.

If you make it through Stage 3, you go to Stage 4, the Systems Stage, where a True Business Is Born. You're going to create and manage systems with the people in the sandbox. You know you're in Stage 4 when you lay out the job descriptions, tasks and processes, and the people already in your structure do them on their own. Every job starts to develop its own personality. Things happen without you.

The pace of your business will actually slow a little bit. You'll come into the office and it will seem calm. Things are running smoothly. You may not be used to this. This is not the fast-paced go, go, go, go, go of Stages 1 and 2. It doesn't mean you're moving more slowly as a business, it means internally, you are running much more efficiently.

Early in Stage 4, you're going to have a very internal focus, because you're building, creating these systems. It's much like when you teach your kids to walk or how to ride a bike; you have your hand by the seat of their pants or the seat of the bicycle, just in case they falter. Your sales might actually dip just a bit, because you're going to spend time on your internal client, which is your employee base.

As you move through the mid to late part of this particular stage, sales will start to grow exponentially, because in the mid part, you're improving the systems. And this is where the Intelligent, Incremental Improvements to Quality (or I³Q) come in. As you improve each one of these systems, the people in it start to improve and, exponentially, sales begin to grow. And, in the latter parts of the stage, your overall quality begins to improve, which leads to the increased sales.

As you begin this culture of Intelligent, Incremental Improvements to Quality, you soon move toward becoming a Stage 5 business. Stage 5 is called the Sustainability Stage, Where a Franchise Is Born. Whether it's formally or informally called a franchise, you are at the point where the systems of your business become the rock star. The systems work in the business; you work *on* the business. The systems run the business; you just oversee them. I³Q becomes the culture.

Look at Starbucks, McDonald's, Southwest Airlines. Look at the types of companies that you go to on a regular basis. These are among the most profitable leaders in their industries. Their cultures are about small, yet incremental, very intelligent improvements to their quality. They have it down to a science. And because they give you that level of certainty and you have a significant experience every time you go there, you're connected to that company.

The average Starbucks patron, given a 20-day work month, goes to Starbucks 18 out of those 20 days, says Joseph Michelli in his book *The Starbucks Experience.* Most of those people will pass by local vendors, stores, delis, diners, where they can cup of coffee for less than $1, on their way to buying a $3-$4 cup of coffee at Starbucks. Why? Because the systems are the star. They no longer are attached to the personality of the owner.

In the same way, your sales continue to grow exponentially. They explode. You are unfairly rewarded on the positive side at this level. After all of the work you've put in, you are now rewarded in spades, and over and over again.

This stage is the first time you can start to think about expansion. In the Sustainability Stage, you can expand, open up new locations, and introduce new products, because your business is now sustainable.

That leads you to Stage 6, the Salability Stage, where An Asset Is Born. Why do people start a business? One of the many reasons is to sell it. When you begin at Stage 1 with Stage 7 in mind, you're designing Stage 1 while thinking of Stage 7. Where am I going to be in five years? That's your vision. You will be starting the business with the succession or sale in mind. You're now a credit-worthy and investor-friendly business. At this point, your focus turns back to sales. The work is rewarding you. Your books look fantastic. This is not a time for overhauling the business.

Ladies will often use the expression that, at this point, it's about "cosmetic" differences, putting on a little lipstick and blush and then heading out. Men will often say, "Just put on a baseball cap, rub on a little deodorant, and we're on our way." This is about cosmetic improvements to the business and then selling it when you reach Stage 7.

If you choose to go through to Stage 7, whether you decide to sell your business or not, it is still part of a Success Cycle to position your company as sellable. In the end, the business is its own being, and likes to become a positive, cash-producing asset. That's what makes it sellable.

Stage 7 is the Succession Stage, where A Legacy Is Born. You're firing on all cylinders. You are an MV²P™ (mission, vision and values, and purpose) business and organization. You have strong direction, robust sales and consistent systems. You have quality products and controls. You can now pass this business along. You can donate, will it or sell it to somebody, or you can keep it as a cash-producing annuity or asset.

That success cycle from Stage 1 through Stage 7 can be a 36-month journey. Follow the methodology, and in 36 months, you can go from start-up to seven figures and be in a position to pass along your business or sell it.

IN CONCLUSION

At every stage of the success cycle, you'll find that there is a common theme. In every stage, you will have an outcome. There will be an area of focus. Then, most important, you will use the 7 Stages power tools for that particular stage to maximize that stage and to stay on track for a success, as you define it in your business.

Business DISCoverY™ Wheel

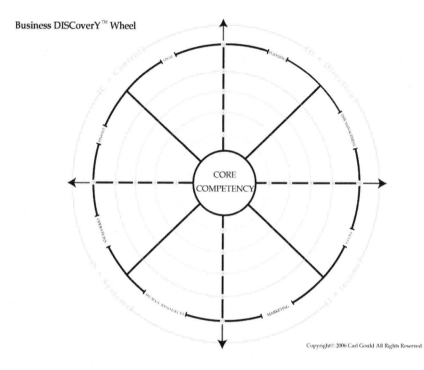

CHAPTER 4:

BLINDNESS, BANKRUPTCY, GETTING IT RIGHT, AND ROCKETS

As I've mentioned, every person has blind spots. Yet **your business cannot have blind spots**: Your competitors will pick you off and your business will fail. Maybe you've already experienced this: You had an incredible vision, but never got your systems in place. You had dynamite sales, but your contracts were full of holes and you never collected all your money.

Don't worry. The average self-made millionaire has been near or in bankruptcy more than three times. They simply learned to fail forward. One of your strongest attributes is your perseverance or what used to be called "stick-to-itiveness." Your willingness to keep trying is what will set you apart from the rest.

One of the keys to building a successful business is building it in the right order. From my observation, most entrepreneurs start in the I and then move to the S of the DISCoverY process. They try to create sales, and then people begin to advise them that they need systems. Then they run and try to implement a system. When things start to fall apart they say, "Whoa, we better get some controls in place, because our sales are suffering. We're losing money." The attempt at controls tends to be too little too late, and so then (and only then) do they realize they need to go back to basics and start planning.

This strategy is like what a lot of people do when they get a model airplane with "some assembly required." They open the package with great excitement, announcing to family members that a wonderful model airplane is forthcoming. They get their tools and take everything out of the box and start putting pieces together. The problem is, now they've used up all the little bolts and there are extra pieces that don't seem to be connected to anything. They begin to realize that it's not going so well, so they undo a few screws and bolts and try reconnecting them in other ways. Maybe they even look for a better set of tools. They realize this isn't going so well, either, so they tighten up the screws a little bit more and maybe get a better screwdriver. They glance at the box and then realize that this is supposed to be assembled in 20 minutes, and they've been working on it for two hours. And that's when they think about looking at the instructions.

That's the way most people try to build a business. They tell the world they're opening soon and then they lay out a system. When that doesn't work so well, they try to rearrange things. Without a plan, how in the world do you know what fits with what, and what you need to control? In the very end, they conclude that they need to go back to the big picture and essentially start over.

It's much easier to start building in the right order from the beginning. Start with the big picture, the D (direction). Your strategy is to sell your business first and create it later, which means your next item of focus is sales, or the I (income). Third, you tackle controls. This translates into solidifying your quality. Once you have very high D, I, C, then, and only then, do you start implementing systems. In a nutshell: Have a big vision. Start selling your vision. Create the quality product. Then implement your systems.

Systems show up in Stage 4. It is very important that you complete Stages 1-3 before implementing strong and rigid systems. We work with thousands of companies around the world at any given time. In this process, we have observed patterns of success and patterns of failure. Time and again we have found that successful businesses build in the order of D, I, C and then S. Plan, sell, create then systemize.

PERSONALITY DEVELOPMENT: STAGES 5 AND 6

As you progress through the 7 Stages, the business is continually developing its own personality. By Stage 5, the business has "cut its umbilical cord" from its owner and displays distinct characteristics all its own.

In these later stages, the systems become the star. You begin to become known for your systems: how you make that perfect ice cream sundae every time; how quickly you seat people in your restaurant; that chocolate on the pillow. Your system should become so efficient that you can now turn your attention to expansion.

In Stage 6 you begin to focus on cosmetic enhancements to the business that further distinguish it from the competition and enhance its unique personality. You will insert vice presidents to run sections of the business. Ideally, these are people you cultivated and can promote from within. You will build sales to make sure your books look great. In Stage 7 you are ready to sell the business or hire a CEO. The business' personality is fully developed and you can move on.

FUNCTIONAL VS. DYSFUNCTIONAL PROBLEMS

Problems are an inescapable part of life, but not all problems indicate the same underlying cause. There are functional problems, which you can reasonably expect will resolve themselves with time and effort, and there are dysfunctional problems, which indicate an underlying flaw that must be addressed. For example, if you are struggling with some aspect of skiing after your second trip to the slopes, that would be a functional problem. No one expects you to know how to ski perfectly without some instruction and a lot of practice. On the other hand, if you couldn't even walk from the car to the ski lodge without running out of breath, that would be a dysfunctional problem. You are seriously out of shape or have an underlying health problem that needs to be dealt with immediately.

Problems, challenges and opportunities will constantly present themselves for your business. You will evaluate each to determine whether it is functional or dysfunctional based on the stage you're in. A functional problem could be any challenge that results from following your plan and will eventually help you get to where you want to go. For example, your life may be a bit out of balance in Stage 2 as you seek to become an expert in your field. You are doing most of the marketing and selling. Your customers love *you* so they want you (not anyone else!) to make the product, deliver the service, perform the follow- ups, and so on. You may also be taking classes to add to your professional credentials. You will be pulled in many directions with very little free time. This is a very functional problem of Stage 2. The reward is that you will be able to increase your fees and expand your customer base. You can't live like this forever, but the short-term inconvenience will yield a long-term gain. A dysfunctional problem, however, indicates an underlying issue that will ultimately take you further away from your goals. For example, procrastination is a dysfunctional problem. By delaying the execution or implementation of a critical task, you have a problem that is bringing you further away from your goals as a BOE. Another dysfunctional problem is to be flush with excess cash in Stage 1 and (early) Stage 2. Sure, you've read that most businesses fail because they are *under*capitalized and run out of cash. But in Stages 1 and 2, you manage your cash very strategically and reinvest it in the business to ensure future growth. The book "The Southwest Airlines Way" explains that one of the key competitive strategies was to purchase fuel in advance and lock in low rates. When fuel prices then increased substantially and began squeezing operations at *other* airlines, Southwest remained profitable with no layoffs. Had it not prepurchased the fuel and remained flush with excess cash, it would have faced the same fate as the other airlines. Southwest continued its aggressive growth throughout this time and has maintained its industry-leading advantage.

When building a business, you'll inevitably face problems at various stages with cash flow, profits, sales, time-management, government regulations and employees. Depending on the stage, they could be functional or dysfunctional. Cash flow, in the early stages of a business, is a functional problem. But if you had an abundance of cash in an early stage, it might indicate a crash ahead, as the airlines example illustrates. We all know that some large corporations make cuts to inflate stock prices that ultimately send the company down the tubes. A small business can do the same thing by failing to spend money on front-end investments in the organization that will give it long-term viability.

On the other hand, take that same symptom of cash flow in the later stages (5, 6 or 7) and it would be very dysfunctional. If you've taken 20 skiing lessons and you are no better than when you started, something is wrong. In the later stages, your cash flow should be consistent, profitable and predictable. You should be able to measure it, project it with reasonable accuracy, and then tweak just a bit here and there in order to align with your planning.

Operations problems in the very early stages of your business are also very functional. As I've mentioned, we don't want to implement systems prematurely. However, if you're still struggling with operations in Stage 6, that's a dysfunctional problem. It indicates that something is wrong on a deeper level.

GETTING IT RIGHT

Fortunately, business is about more than just problems. The funny thing is, most of us know when we get something wrong in our personal lives as well as in our business. You make what you think is a joke, and your spouse looks horrified. You try a marketing strategy and sales stay flat. It may not feel great, but it's not complicated.

On the other hand, we don't always know when we get something right, and that, too, can hinder our growth. We may not always lock into the causal factors in our success, and so we don't always know what to keep doing. One of the most significant functions of the DISCoverY process is alerting you when you have gotten it right. That lets you build on success.

Imagine that you have a house you are about to sell. There is no particular pressure to sell quickly, but obviously sooner would be better than later. You inquire with experts — an estate agent or a real estate broker — about the right asking price. They do an analysis and tell you to sell for $100,000. They assure you that if you put it on the market for $100,000, it will sell quickly and you will get very close to your asking price.

So you list the property for $100,000. That very day you sell to the first caller for exactly $100,000. So, you've taken the advice of the experts, put it on the market, and the very first person on the very first day says "I'll take it," and offers you your asking price. Did you ask the right or wrong price?

Let me give you a second scenario. You're selling the same house. You go to the same experts and get the same advice: Ask $100,000 and you'll sell quickly and get close to the asking price. Again, you put your house on the market for $100,000. One year goes by. Two years go by. No one calls or expresses interest. Have you asked the right or wrong price?

In scenario two, it's easy to see you asked the wrong price. Nothing happened the way the experts said. You didn't sell quickly (or at all) and you certainly didn't get close to the asking price.

Now, what about the first scenario? Did your inner skeptic say, "Never take the first offer. It sold too quickly. We could have gotten more."? Yet from a business-building perspective, you absolutely asked the right price. You took all the information you had, consulted experts, made a plan, set a goal and met your expectations. You sold it quickly and you got your asking price. You used the best information available.

This is an example of a sound decision for which you deserve a pat on the back. Could you do better the next time? Of course you could. But you still got it right, and you need to know that.

Knowing when you get it right is very important: You build a successful business on the positive, doing more of what you've gotten right, not less of what you've gotten wrong. The DISCoverY process will show you what you're getting right at every step and every stage of the Success Cycle. The more of your time you invest in what you're getting right, the faster you will go through the cycle.

You can take any business from start-up to seven figures in three years or less. Start-up to Stage 4 takes approximately 18 months. The moment you enter Stage 4, it's another 18 months all the way to Stage 7.

Suppose you're already a seven-figure business and you want to get to ten figures. The numbers change at this point. It typically takes seven to ten years to go from seven to ten figures: 3½-5 years up to Stage 4, and 3½-5 years from Stage 4-7. The principles are the same. Either way, you get there by building on getting it right.

EASY AS ROCKET SCIENCE

I was speaking once to a group of entrepreneurs without realizing we had a rocket scientist in the audience. Naturally, that would be the time I quipped, "Come on, folks. This is not rocket science. Building a business is very simple and systematic."

The rocket scientist raised his hand and said, "I have a correction for you. I am a rocket scientist and let me tell you that business is very much like rocket science. Building and launching a business *is* rocket science." He explained his analogy further.

The working principle for launching a rocket is thrust divided by mass equals lift.

$$\frac{\text{THRUST}}{\text{MASS}} = \text{LIFT}$$

In terms of physics, thrust is the force pushing you forward (or upward), mass is the weight of the object, and lift is the net rise into the sky.

In the business world, thrust is the energy you give to your marketplace: the amount of power and passion with which you serve your clients and please your customer base.

What is mass? Mass is the amount of internal strife or misalignment in the business: the infighting and discontent that is weighing you down. This drains the energy that could be going to your customers. Obviously you want to minimize the amount of energy directed internally so you can direct the most energy outward to your clients.

Lift is results. What results are you committed to? What are the results you're getting? More thrust and less mass equal more lift, or more bang for your buck.

This is where size matters. If you have a little bit of alignment, you get a little bit of lift. If you have a lot of alignment, you get big lift. To maximize lift in the launch of your business, you want to become what I call an MV²P™ organization. How do you accomplish that? You complete the Stage 1 planning that I've laid out for you. This will help you become an aligned, resolved organization based on your ultimate mission, vision, values and purpose. The more aligned you are, the more lift you will get. Business truly is rocket science: very simple.

CHAPTER 5:

UNDERSTANDING THE FOUR STYLES

MV²P™: UNDERSTANDING YOUR PERSONALITY STYLE

I n the DISCoverY process, we build a successful business by aligning behaviors, vision, values and attributes to our MV²P Planning™. MV²P™ stands for Mission, Vision and Values, and Purpose.

Why are our mission, vision, values and purpose so important? They are important because you must have buy-in from your employees before you can sell. They must understand and own the mission, vision, values and purpose of the company, so that their behavior aligns with them. This alignment regarding what is most important to everyone in the company leaves more energy to focus outward on the customer. If you spend all day bickering over what your priorities are or why you are in business, your customers will suffer.

As you're going through your MV²P Planning™, it's very important to remain conscious of your personality type as well as those of your staff. This helps you understand office dynamics and maximize your flexibility, especially in the early stages. During the first three of the seven stages, flexibility reigns supreme. In Stages 4 through 7, the controls and systems take over for good. At the beginning, however, you'll need all your patience and then some.

PATTERNS OF THE FOUR PERSONALITIES

What do these four styles look like in day-to-day interactions? What observable behavior does each generate? First of all, each style draws you toward certain industries and positions and away from others. It is important to note that your personal style has nothing to do with your potential, your intelligence, or your value as a human being. There is no "good" or "bad" style or "right" or "wrong" style. It is simply a lens through which we can observe and understand how you operate during the course of the day.

Remember that you are a product of both genetics and environment. You were born and wired a certain way, and throughout the course of your life, you have responded to the conditions around you. You conditioning, however, will dictate that you go in certain directions.

Research has shown that the average person has approximately 40,000 thoughts per day. Ninety-five percent of those thoughts are the same as those of the day before.[3] We are creatures of habit and we tend to live out the results of our conditioning on a day-to-day basis. Your conditioning is probably the leading cause of stress, frustration and anger in your business and life. The DISCoverY process can help correct this, and get your new business off on the right foot.

OUT OF SYNCH

Have you ever heard someone say, "I am becoming my mother" or "my father"? Depending on his relationship with that parent, he might be proud or exasperated about the discovery. We tend to follow in the

---

3 Deepak Chopra as interviewed on *"Power Talk"* www.TonyRobbins.com.

footsteps of those who came before us, not always because we want to, but rather because we feel obligated. This often results in an individual who chooses a profession by responding her environment and not necessarily her true nature. If you feel burned out, stressed, resentful or fearful, it's probably because your current position is not aligning with your true nature.

A client of mine whom I will call Peter was working as an attorney when I began to coach him. He possessed a high I people-oriented personality style: He was full of optimism and trust, loved a fast-paced life, and gave little attention to detail. The legal industry is a C industry: obsessed with detail, and characterized by a methodical pace, task completion, and little human interaction.

To do his job well, Peter was adapting his behavior to its demands, despite the fact that this went against everything inside him. Not being true to your core nature is like holding your breath: Eventually you must exhale. Peter was at that point of exhaling when we began working together. After a decade of working in a profession for which he was ill suited, he was exhausted, beleaguered with chronic health challenges, and facing a failed marriage. All this was before his 40th birthday.

Peter's dilemma was that he loved the law but hated being a lawyer. A huge case load, countless arguments and contracts, and long hours of research with only chance personal interactions left him drained and discouraged. Like so many of my clients, Peter started judging himself incompetent and worthless for showing shortcomings in a profession he despised. In his mind, he had no right to complain: He had a great salary and a successful practice. Inwardly, he felt like a loser.

I helped Peter apply the DISCoverY Process and 7 Stage thinking to his dilemma, and helped him face his situation with some introspection and a good dose of honesty. Peter admitted that he chose his career because he came from a long line of attorneys and was expected to follow suit. He responded by excelling in school, passing the bar exam, and going into practice. The only problem was that being a lawyer made him miserable. Unfortunately, his unhappiness in his job soon spilled over into other areas of his life: His health and his relationships began falling apart as well. Peter consulted doctors for his health and therapists for his relationships, but it was only after he admitted he needed to change his overall direction that things began to turn for him.

Peter created a vision for his life (Stage 1). He realized that though he hated his day-to-day activities, he wanted to stay in the law. He identified the areas that he enjoyed and created a plan to work in those areas. Then he identified a key passion: He loved interacting with people. He shifted the focus of his practice, retaining only a few of his existing clients (the ones he liked, of course!) and referred the rest to other law firms. He then started a consulting practice that helped fellow attorneys and others in the legal profession succeed in their businesses and find balance between life and work.

Now Peter humorously refers to himself as a "recovering attorney" and he could not be happier. He interacts with people every day knowing that he is having a significant impact in their lives. For the first time in his life, Peter knows he is really at the helm of his ship. His work is harmonious with his nature and it feels effortless.

The DISCoverY process helps you align your strategies with your personality. This will make all your responsibilities more enjoyable and less tedious. Every job, just like every person, has an underlying emotional pattern. For example, those choleric D people are passionate and driven. On the other hand, the sanguine I people are full of optimism. No matter what's going on, they are always walking on the sunny side of the street. Your phlegmatic S people will show very little emotion until they are completely comfortable with their surroundings and relationships. They prefer to focus on the impersonal world of structure and find great comfort in the predictable.

Lastly, your melancholic compliants often display the emotional pattern of fear. The C people tend to move very slowly and cautiously, considering all possible repercussions of their actions before making a decision.

Your conditioning will lead you to an industry that has one of these underlining emotional patterns, which may or may not align with your true nature. As you become aware of that nature, you will find your career choices resonate with a deeper part of yourself. This will ultimately reduce your stress and frustration and you will have a much more fulfilling experience in whatever you do.

INDUSTRIES OF THE FOUR PERSONALITY TYPES

Every individual has elements of all four personality types, and every company needs people with strengths in each area. However, certain industries attract one personality type over the others. Some examples of D (Dominant) companies include Microsoft, General Electric, ExxonMobil and the Virgin companies. These are pioneering organizations that take a lot of risks. A company that drills for oil in the middle of the ocean or carves through miles of ice to explore for resources is putting a lot on the line. D companies make up a small percentage of all businesses. They pave the way and the rest of us follow.

An I company could be not only a sales-and-marketing-type (auto dealerships, real estate agencies, etc.) company, but also a multi-level marketing company such as Mary Kay Cosmetics, a media organization, or even a daytime talk show.

The S companies and industries rely on schedules, on-time performance and consistency. The military, law enforcement and firefighting fields, educational organizations, government agencies, and transportation industries all fit this mold. They must be very consistent, reliable and predictable to be successful.

Lastly we have our C (or Compliant) companies. These include legal services, banking, insurance, financial services, technology, accounting, medicine, engineering and architecture.

Notice that, although technology industries attract high C people, I listed Microsoft as a high D company. Dominant companies can come from many different industries when they are pioneers. It is easier to describe the other three (I, S and C) as industries with distinct characteristics. D companies tend to stand out and must often be examined individually.

WHEN TO TAKE OFF

Once you decide what type of business fits your personality, how do you begin? According to the Small Business Administration, more than 50% of small businesses fail in the first year and 95% fail within the first five years.[4] Yet a 1999 study by the United States Chamber of Commerce found that 86% of franchises opened within the last five

---

4 "Are You Ready?" United States Small Business
Administration: http://www.sba.gov/starting_business/startup/areyouready.html

years were still under the same ownership and 97% of them were still open for business.[5] What is the difference between an independent business and a franchise that makes their success rates so drastically different?

If you answered "systems," you are absolutely right. A successful system makes a successful company. This is one of the most overlooked areas in business. Yet structure comes before systems. This holds true even if you buy a system (i.e. a franchise) before you open your doors. In practical terms, structure means putting the right people in the right roles with the right tasks.

In the beginning, you are not controlling 100% of everything your employees do. They must be able to serve clients with minimal training, using their initiative and flexibility. In this process, you will begin to develop your systems.

In the same way, there is a checklist to follow every time a plane takes off. Before the pilot can implement the "system" of takeoff, there is a structure for takeoff known as the "standard day." This describes the ideal conditions of weather, weight and wind for putting that plane in the air. There is a very specific structure needed to get that plane off the ground. In reality, however, if the pilot waited for that ideal day to come around — the standard day —we'd be waiting on that runway for six to nine months.

Naturally, the pilot has to exercise his or her good judgment to determine when the plane and the conditions are safe for flying.

---

5 Source: http://www.franchiseconsultantsinc.com/statistics.html

Many business owners, on the other hand, will wait for the ideal day in order to take off, hoping they don't run out of fuel or provisions in the process. That standard day comes around a few times a year. In order to get that plane in the air, the pilot makes adjustments, using common sense and experience. What has he or she done in the past to get this plane into the air safely? Once the pilot has done that, he or she can then implement the system: the autopilot. Then the pilot merely adjusts course as needed.

The plane can't leave the ground on autopilot, and your business can't take off on the basis of systems. You must have a structure first. Systems will then follow.

THE RIGHT PERSON IN THE RIGHT JOB

If structure means the right person in the right place, how do you *know* you have the right person in the right place? Their true natures, experiences, attributes, and skills line up with their job descriptions. Performing their tasks gives them energy, instead of draining them.

If doing their jobs energizes people, you have the right structure and people. You'll put the systems in later to help everyone grow within the organization. At the beginning, your focus is putting people who are enthusiastic about what they are doing into the right jobs.

DISCOVERY MIRROR™

You must capitalize on your strengths in order to get your business off the ground, which is why it must mirror your personality and your strengths. The strengths of the owner become strengths of the business. Look at the diagram at www.the7stages.com/mirror. Notice that it's a circle with four quadrants. The upper right-hand corner is the D (the direction, dominance). The bottom right-hand corner is the I (the income, influential part of you). The bottom left-hand corner is the systems (S), and top left-hand corner is the controls (C).

You'll notice there are two diagonal arrows that run between the D to the S, and between the I and the C. The quadrants diagonal from each other are somewhat adversarial in nature, so strength in one may indicate a blind spot in the other. In other words, if you're very strong at direction, you may struggle in the area of systems. It can be your blind spot. It may not be what you enjoy. If you're strong in systems, you may struggle with big-picture planning. You'll focus on the little things and won't always nurture the overall vision. Likewise, if you are strong in sales and marketing, your blind spot may be controls, and visa versa.

Let's say our business is making a lot of money so our I departments are going strong. Yet not everyone is celebrating. The C departments complain, "We're losing too much. We're making too many mistakes. Had we just planned this out a little bit more, we could have charged more."

Now, if you're strong in controls, you'll cross every "t" and dot every "i," but you may struggle in the area of sales. Chances are, you have trouble letting go and empowering your sales staff. If your company provides a service, you can't know everything about your clientele before you get going. You will have to put yourself out there when things are less than perfect.

Understanding these dynamics will help you create the structure you need to launch. Even though that "standard day" may never come along, your structure will help ensure you get to cruising altitude safely and soundly.

Business DISCoverY™ Wheel

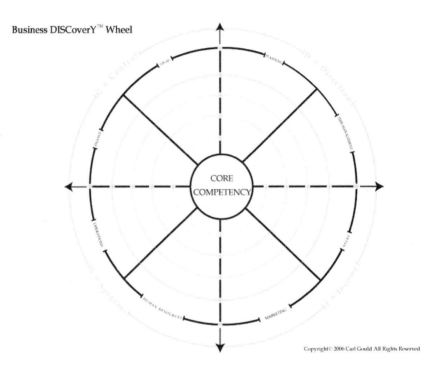

Copyright© 2006 Carl Gould All Rights Reserved

CHAPTER 6:

BUILDING ON STRENGTH

In the business DISCoverY process, there are three areas of discovery. There are your behaviors, which we call the DISC (How you do what you do). There are the values (the Y, motivators, priorities). And there are the attributes, meaning what you will do. You need to discover your strengths and blind spots in these three areas and then align with the mission, vision, values and purpose of the company. That's when you know you have an aligned organization.

Most sports have a regular season that leads into the playoffs. Everything intensifies during the playoffs. That unstoppable defense can become even more impenetrable, but that weak foul-shooter gets sent to the line even more often. The strengths and weaknesses of a team or a player become magnified in the intense environment.

A successful television actor lands her first big-screen role. Now her brilliant sense of comic timing seems 10 times wittier, but her limited range of facial subtlety becomes a problem when it never seemed one before.

Just like moving from the regular season to the playoffs or from the small screen to the big screen, you'll find your strengths and blind spots magnified on the road to becoming this MV²P™ organization. You will become stronger as you build on your strengths. However, if you ignore your blind spots, they will widen and cause you tremendous dysfunctional problems later on.

Remember, you build a business on what you get right. You build on strength. Another area might look like a weakness, compared with your strength, but it can just as easily be thought of as an area of improvement. It's a signal to help you create your "to-do" list, not a value judgment on you or your business.

LOOK IN THE MIRROR

As an entrepreneur, you are probably more of a generalist. To make it this far, you have had to be not only technically savvy in your specialty, but also sufficiently skilled in enough areas to actually start a business. That's why you need a "mirror": somebody who can show you the entire picture. This person needs to be emotionally neutral, not your spouse or a family member.

Some people would call this a coach, a mentor or an advisor. You might even hire a consultant who has a particular skill in an area. This person is casually indifferent to your feelings, because he or she has such a high level of specific skill and sees no need to coddle you any more than a football coach coddles his players. Fixing a particular kind of problem or challenge is what this person does every single day.

The more mirrors you have around you, the more your strengths will grow and actually minimize your blind spots.

Most of us have built up a certain degree of arm strength by lifting and carrying things in our daily routine. Our auxiliary muscles, however, may not get as strong. Now, suppose you start lifting free weights to bulk up your arms. Your arms will get stronger, and in the process you unconsciously recruit help from other muscles. Your weightlifting not only strengthens your arms, but also builds your back, side and neck muscles. Every other area of your body that has to support your exercise gets stronger too.

This same process takes place when you build your business by focusing on your strengths. You work those strengths, recruiting whatever is necessary to get the job done. Then other areas will build up in the process.

DISCOVERY ORGANIZATIONAL CHART™

Once you've recruited your "mirror"/mentor, you're in Stage 3, the Synergy Stage. You will place more people into the structure and then create the systems. The DISCoverY Organizational Chart™ is about to become your new best friend.

The chart, illustrated on www.the7stages.com/orgchart, is a very simple organizational chart. In the beginning, especially, we want to keep everything on one page. The sole exercise we give your for this process will revolutionize your business.

You'll notice that you are at the top: You're the CEO of Me Inc. On the left side are all the activities that bring in customers and cash. That's the D and I side of the organizational chart. On the right side are the S and C parts: that's everything that keeps cash and customers in.

Along the bottom is a large box full of lines. For the next two weeks, catalogue in brutal detail everything you do in that space. Be honest with yourself. Write down every task that you do and how long it takes you to complete it. This is the most accurate way to create an appropriate structure for your business. It forces you to confront which tasks you can delegate and which you cannot. Soon, you will start organizing these tasks and handing them off to others.

You want to be very specific in this process. Avoid generalizing: Got mail, took 10 minutes. You want lists like this: Walked to the post office to get the mail: two minutes; retrieved mail: one minute; sorted the mail: three minutes; distributed the mail to the appropriate people: two minutes; answered my mail: eight minutes. Once you have all these seemingly minuscule tasks listed, you will ask whether each activity brings in or keeps in new customers and cash. When you've answered that question, you will "file" each task on either the right or left side of the box.

Next, put your name in the upper blanks on both sides as well. You are the vice president of sales and marketing as well as the vice president of operations. And, on the top, again, that's you, the CEO of Me Inc. No wonder you're so tired!

CEO/BOE - ('BUSINESS OWNER ENTREPRENEUR')

This side **brings** it in   This side **keeps** it in

DIRECTION 'D' Big Picture	INCOME 'I' Sales & Marketing	SYSTEMS 'S' Operations	CONTROLS 'C' Detail
Planning Activities	Sales & Marketing Activities	Day-to-Day Activities	Technology, Checks & Balances

This exercise helps you accomplish something very important: You have now created detailed job descriptions for every role in the business, and right now your name is above every single one. Soon, working with your strategic partner, you will fire yourself from each job every quarter for the first 18 months. That will get you to Stage 4.

Thereafter, the firing process continues until your name is in only one box: the CEO. You will know you've hit Stage 7 when you actually fire yourself from that position and hire a new CEO, who will run the business just as well if not better than you. That's when your legacy is born.

After you've filled out your DISCoverY Organizational Chart™, you can begin delegating or hiring. You will begin at the bottom of the chart and work your way up. Start delegating the basic tasks and move on to the more managerial ones. As you hire others and fire yourself from various jobs, you'll see those boxes with your name fill with the names of your employees.

During this process, you will imprint your personality on each position. Your business will be developing its own unique culture and qualities based on your individuality. You might be slow and methodical or fast and spontaneous. Either way, each part of the business begins to take on those characteristics. As you begin to create structure for the organization, you should feel at home in every department. No matter what anyone else tells you, you must be able to live with the structural decisions you make. They must fit your goals but they must also fit your personality.

MATCHING PEOPLE TO THEIR STYLES

When you fill those boxes on your organizational chart, you will be matching people's styles with their positions. Fortunately, most people gravitate toward the job that they're already good at, whether they realize it or not. Most of us enjoy doing something we are skilled at and are skilled at what we like doing.

One of the best strategies when interviewing individuals is to show them a list of tasks and ask them which of those tasks they enjoy. They will almost always choose what they do best.

The other key in the hiring process is to be able to share your vision for the company with prospective hires. You've already done this with the advisors you've brought on board. Now you need to share with your employees where they will fit within the "big picture." This will help them buy into the overall direction of the organization, and gravitate to the roles they will fill best.

VALUES: THE "WHY"

Next on the list in the DISCoverY process are your values. Why is it important that you're in this business? What motivates you? What do you want motivating your employees? These values are the glue that not only holds the relationships within the business together but also the relationships between customers and the company.

The values are the Y in the DISCoverY process. They reflect what is most important and urgent to us. Aligning our behavior with our priorities will reduce our stress and frustration and increase our fulfillment and happiness. Your company's mission must be in alignment with who you consider yourself to be. If an option or a person aligns with the mission of the business, they're right for the business. If they don't align with business, they are not.

Values shape both our decisions and our priorities. They determine how we spend our money, our time and our energy. According to author Edward Spranger, human beings have six basic categories of motivators, indicative of their values. For a full description of these six categories of motivators, go to www.the7stages.com/assessments, take a Priorities Assessment, and learn your values hierarchy.

ATTRIBUTES

We've covered the "how" (behaviors) and the "why" (values) of your business. Now it's time to examine the "what." These are your attributes. What are the qualities that make up your personality? What are you good at? What do you want to do? Your personal attributes will determine your role within the company. Remember that our goal in the DISCoverY process is to make the behaviors, values and attributes align with your mission, vision, values and purpose.

This sounds like a daunting task, but it is actually very simple. You do you Stage 1 planning with your MV^{2}P™ planning in mind. You hire your mentor-mirror and then you will find that the attributes, values and behaviors fall right into place. You've created a very clear vision of your company and your certainty about that vision causes others to gravitate toward it. You clearly define the roles and tasks so that people know what they're getting into and you can effectively manage their expectations. Just like the model airplane, you're giving everyone the directions ahead of time so that you all know what you're building together.

To better understand your attributes and learn your Personal Power Indicator™, go to www.the7stages.com.

SUMMARY: DISCOVERY PROCESS

The most important principle in the business DISCoverY process is that you must know yourself. You're the one leading this venture and the buck stops with you. Then, based on your knowledge of yourself, you need to determine what's right for your business. Once you've done that, you can bring in the people who are right for that business. Put the right people in the right jobs, doing their tasks for all the right reasons. These are people whose values will align with the values of the company and who will be motivated to work every day with enthusiasm. These are the people who will help make that vision a reality.

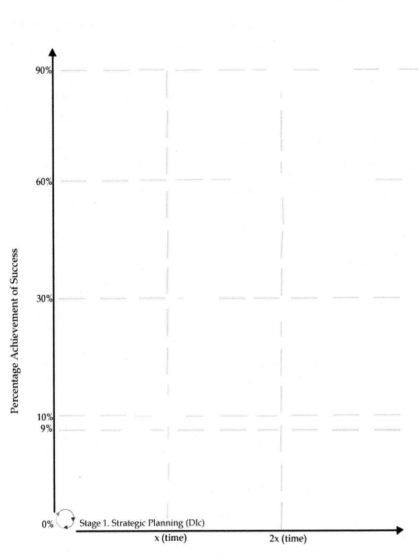

THE STRATEGIC PLANNING STAGE

"A Dream Is Born"

INTRODUCTION

Welcome to Stage 1! The Strategic Planning Stage is all about designing your future. Your personal drive will determine how fast you move through this stage. Your ultimate goal is to persuade the marketplace that you have a good idea for a product or service. This is the stage where you capture your dream on paper. You will articulate the benefits of your product and the mission of your enterprise in such a way that people will buy into your idea. You actually have to sell it before you create it: pretty risky! In essence, you are making a promise you know you can deliver by Stage 2 and beyond. This is all based on your Stage 1 planning, which is why it is so critical to the long-term viability of your company. The business can grow only to the size of your vision. The business will NOT grow beyond your vision. This is the time to dream HUGE, think BIG, and play the game smartly. Your strongest, best and most valuable asset as an entrepreneur is your capacity to dream (i.e. your vision). It must be nurtured and guarded at all costs.

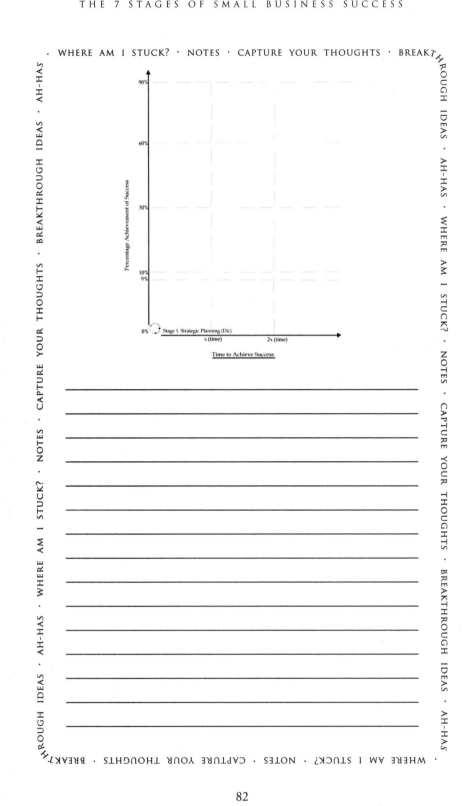

Your blind spot during this stage is your systems: You don't know how they will work yet, because they don't exist. That means you are vulnerable to other companies that already have systems. There are companies out there right now that can take advantage of your ideas and bring them to market more easily and faster than you can in Stage 1. That is why you must make absolutely certain that you complete your MV²P™ Planning and articulate a clear vision for the company.

Many companies have started out with a brilliant product that they later lost because they lacked this clear vision. The creator of the disk operating system, or DOS, was a brilliant guy with no vision. He sold it to Bill Gates and Paul Allen of Microsoft for $50,000, and I don't have to tell you what happened next. Xerox Corporation developed the mouse and the operating system that now powers the Macintosh. The LCD technology for digital watches came originally from Switzerland, but Japan brought it to unprecedented mass production. General Motors pioneered the small-block eight-cylinder engine decades ago, but didn't know what to do with it. Land Rover did.

And the list goes on. Have you ever had a great idea but not known what to do with it, only to learn that someone else brought it to market? It is not a question of skill; it is a question of vision. Vision drives you, and then leads to results.

Lack of vision and a clear plan will cause you to give up on your dream only to have someone else realize it. In business parlance, "without a clear vision, a business will perish." If it is too small or hasn't been committed to paper, your vision stands little chance of survival. Heed these stories as warnings of what can happen when we fail to maximize Stage 1.

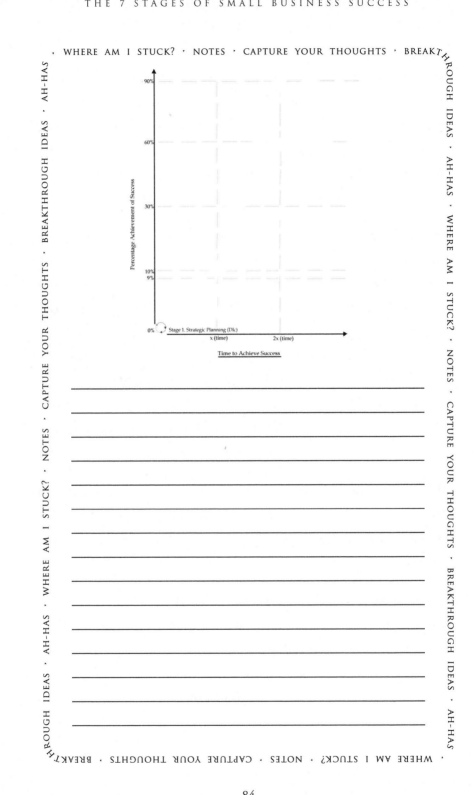

To deal with the reality of having no systems, most entrepreneurs end up creating enough structure to manage day-to-day operations. Then they buckle down and do whatever it takes to get to that first customer. It is vital to maintain maximum flexibility during this stage: Having a simple structure allows you to get the business off the ground, secure some customers, and begin making money.

Speaking of money, the largest challenge during Stage 1 is cash flow, or lack thereof. You have very few, if any, sales. So in absence of a business loan, investment capital or independent wealth, money will probably be a headache during this stage.

In this chapter, we'll focus on the great part of Stage 1: your power tools. I call these tools MV²P™ decisions: Mission, Vision, Values, and Purpose. These are the foundational aspects of your business that you can establish in Stage 1 that will be very hard to tinker with once your business is up and running. In many ways, starting a business is like getting married. You put a ton of planning into the wedding day and it is almost always very successful. The flowers, cake, music and so on are just as you planned. Typically, much less planning goes into the actual marriage. According to the National Center for Health Statistics, a division of the CDC, which is part of the U.S. Dept. of Health and Human Services 48% of marriages end in divorce. I often wonder how many more marriages would be successful in the long run if the partners prepared for the relationship and not just the wedding. Through the activities in this chapter, ongoing assessments, and by utilizing a strategic partner, you will find Stage 1 is both exciting and rewarding.

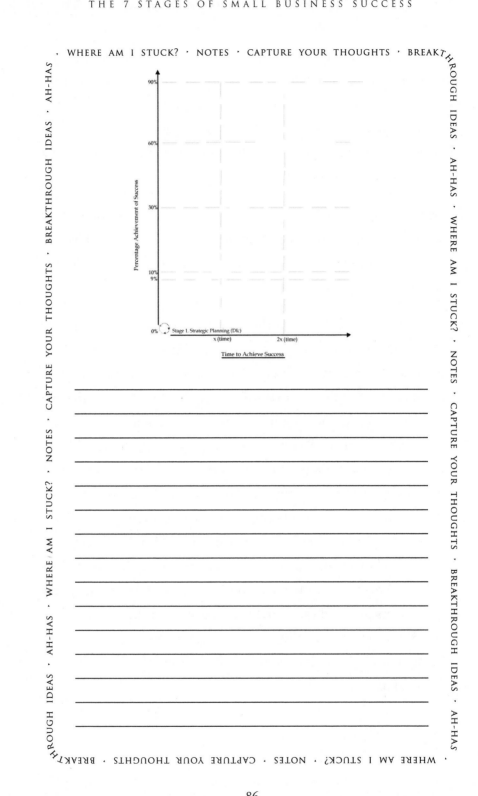

A DREAM IS BORN

Why start a business? Why leave the security of a 9-to-5 job to risk a life where the buck stops with you? There are a lot of reasons, and I shared some of mine in the Introduction. Most start a business with a dream. The Strategic Planning Stage is where you make sure that dream doesn't turn into a nightmare!

In reality, most of you BOEs don't always think these things through. You tend to be impulsive, decisive and strong-willed. A BOE will make snap decisions based on his mood and problem of the moment: ready, fire, and then aim!

To the business owner, everything is an opportunity. So you make a decision in two minutes and abandon it two seconds. You are resourceful people with a competitive streak: You don't just play games, you win games. What's more, you will seek out games you know you can win. If you sense you are falling behind, you are not afraid to cut your losses.

Strategic Planning is a way of seeking out the game you can win. It is a road map to success. Have you ever gotten directions on the Internet? At minimum, you have to provide the starting point and the ending point for your journey. If you are able to give only an approximate destination, then the service can give you only vague directions.

Most of us have found that vague directions make for a frustrating trip: You have no idea whether you're headed the right way, whether you're making good time, or how much longer you'll be on the road. If you've got kids in the back seat, you'll be hearing, "Are we there yet?" quite a bit.

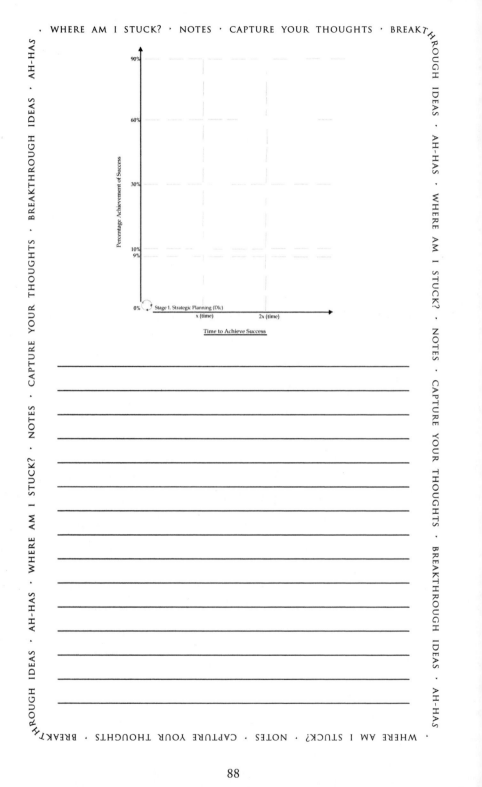

Stage 1. Strategic Planning (Dlc)

_____

_____

_____

_____

_____

_____

_____

_____

_____

_____

_____

_____

During the Strategic Planning Stage, you need to know your precise starting point and the exact destination for your business. You will also need to have a team of navigators monitoring your progress, much like a GPS system, to make sure you stay on the right track. This is not just for start-ups: Existing businesses that decide to launch a new product or division or re-brand their products often find it beneficial to revisit the Strategic Planning Stage.

SELL FIRST, BUILD LATER

Just like a road trip, effective planning takes time on the front end, but saves time and money in the long run. It is also essential to the "sell first, build later" strategy that is increasingly popular in the business world.

Consider the PSL, a personal seat license, which sports venues sell to fans before the stadium is ever built. You actually purchase the right to buy the seat prior to the construction of the stadium or arena. Once the edifice is standing, you can purchase the seat if you choose. Apple presold the iPod® and the iPhone® very successfully. Day traders make millions selling stock options. Franchisors around the world sell their franchise concepts to entrepreneurs, while builders and developers sell homes and rental space based on the blueprints.

Why would you buy a house, a business, a car, or a seat in a stadium that you cannot see or touch? At first glance, you've bought nothing more than a piece of paper. Yet in reality, you bought into the mission, vision, values and purpose of the organization. You've bought the plan for the house, the concept of the phone, or the business plan of the franchise. What compelled you to make such a significant investment

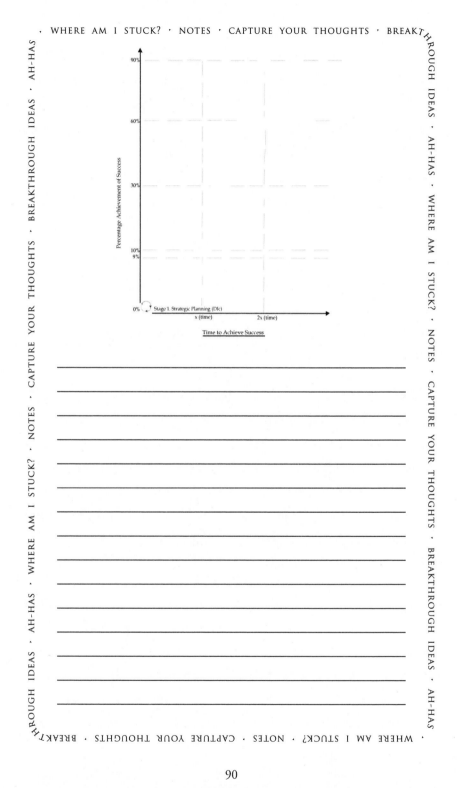

in a product or service that does not yet exist? It was the BOE's vision, passion and enthusiasm. Not only that, his plan sounded great; when he explained it to you, you saw your name was written all over it.

Now I promise you that the BOE did not feel like writing everything down. Most entrepreneurs love to dream but hate anything that involves pen and paper. Yet he fought through the resistance, thought through the launch of the business thoroughly, and captured his hopes, dreams and objectives on paper. In short, he completed his Stage 1 Strategic Planning and became an MV²P™ organization. He articulated the mission, vision, values and purpose for his company, creating a plan that was mutually beneficial for you and for him.

Businesses operate on one of two planes: the competitive plane or the creative plane. On the competitive plane, you are literally fighting with other businesses for the same customers and the same dollars. On the creative plane, you produce something new or perfect an existing product or service. When you operate on the creative plane, customers seek *you* out. The iPod® and iPhone® are two clear examples of Apple's ability to bring something new and different to an already crowded electronics market.

Operating on the creative plane means you are dreaming bigger and bolder than anyone else in the industry. When the iPod® was created, its tag line was "1,000 songs in your pocket." That was an absurd and unreasonable objective. Now "1,000 songs in your pocket" is the rule, not the exception. The vision was so big and bold that millions and millions bought into the idea, the product and the associated service (iTunes®).

Isn't it better to be on the creative plane where there is no competition? Write your plan in a way that generates forward movement and

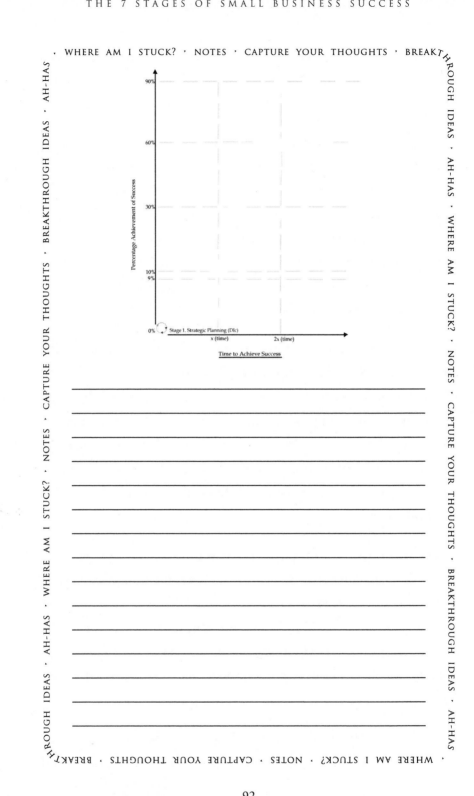

inspires others. For an example of awe-inspiring plans and templates, visit www.the7stages.com/plans.

Starbucks is an example of a company that took an existing product and created a new market for it. It was able to sell not just coffee, but the experience of coming to a coffeehouse. If you complete the activities described below, you can take your company to the creative plane during Stage 1.

DESIGNING THE FUTURE

The outcome of Stage 1 is the design of your future. You start by utilizing your 7-Stage Power Tools™; designing your mission, vision, values and purpose statement. You also complete your business, marketing and sales plans, and list the milestones you intend to strike along the way. Let's take these one by one:

How do you design a **mission statement**? The mission statement answers the question "Why does this business exist?" It explains what you are here to do and whom you are here to serve. It shows what is unique about your product, service or idea. For templates and instructions to create a compelling mission statement, go to www.the7stages. com/plans.

A **vision statement** answers the question "Where will we be in five, 10, or 20 years?" A vision statement paints a picture of the future of the company in terms of finances, personnel, market share, and other key achievements and qualities.

Your **values statement** expresses how you hope your business will be remembered. What are you here to contribute? Once your customers

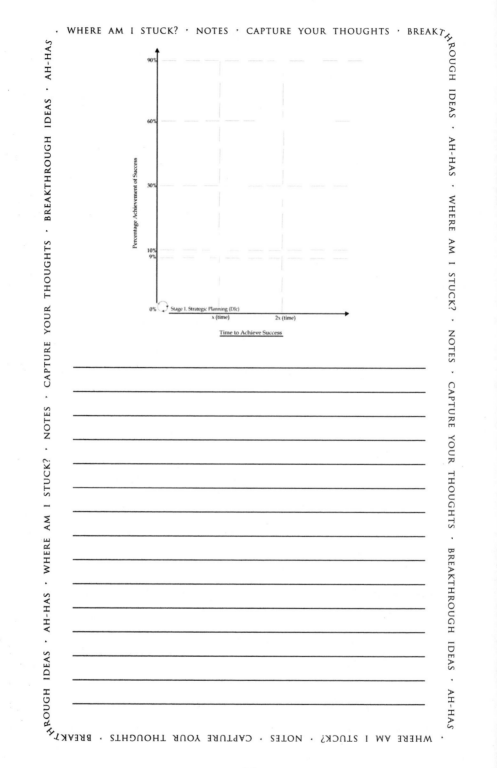

Percentage Achievement of Success

90%

60%

30%

10%
9%

0%   Stage 1. Strategic Planning (Dlc)

x (time)   2x (time)

Time to Achieve Success

THE STRATEGIC PLANNING STAGE

have purchased your service or product, it should improve their lives in a measurable way. The values statement articulates your priorities and what you stand for.

The **business plan** details more the "nuts and bolts" of your product, service or idea. It names your customers, market and competition. It discusses the physical location of operations, strategy for advertising and marketing, as well as your unique selling proposition. The business plan answers questions like "How large will your company become and just how long do you plan to stay in business?" It also addresses details such as corporate structure, board membership, the executive team, operating on a fiscal or calendar year, costs and profit margins. It outlines the strategies that will govern your overall operations and the tactics you'll use to implement those strategies. It will list all the specific tasks that will need to be completed at each stage of the company's development, the position descriptions for each employee, and even their salaries.

Once you've written your business plan, you will need to formulate your **marketing plan**. The marketing plan will outline how you will advertise and launch your product and promote the product name. It details the characteristics of your ideal customer, as well as broader qualities of the company, such as your message, brand and image. While writing your marketing plan, you'll determine how many prospective customers you need to generate, look at your advertising budget, and determine what type of media will help you meet your goals. You'll also have to start laying the foundation for systems by outlining customer follow-up policies and procedures. After all that, you decide specific activities to list on your marketing calendar in order to make sure you meet your goals.

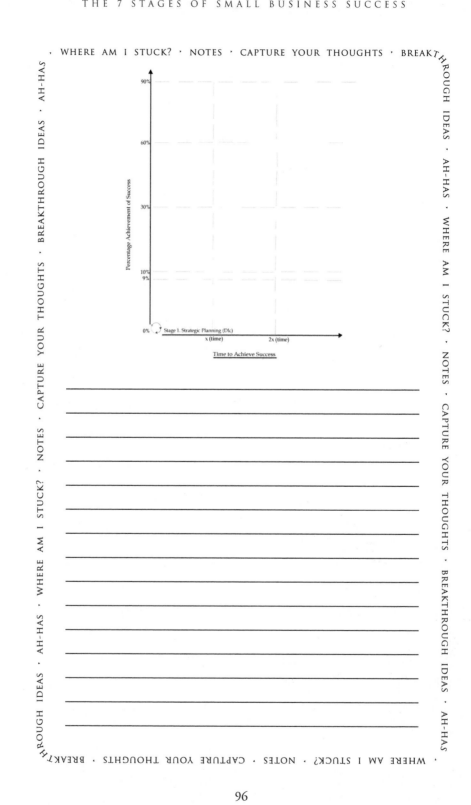

The number of customers you expect to reach can help you outline your **sales plan**. How much income do you need to generate on a regular basis in order to survive and cover your monthly overheads? What income level will enable your business to thrive? The answers to these questions tell you the goals for your sales plan, which outlines your policies, procedures and methodology. From identifying the sales staff, to making a prospective customer a repeat customer, the sales plan has it all. It also details how the sales force will be compensated and how the individual and team goals will be set.

Once these plans are in place, it's time to list specific measurable **goals** for yourself and your business. You set achievement goals for specific ranges of time, from weeks to months to quarters and years. You set these for yourself as the BOE, as well as your executive team members.

During Stage 1, you must take the time to complete a goal-setting exercise to write out your short-term and long-term goals. You will never maximize the efficiency of your daily activities if you are not conscious of your short- and long-term objectives. This will help you work smarter, rather than harder.

Next, you'll do your **milestone planning**. This is distinct from goal-setting (commitment to an activity) in that it is a commitment to achievement regardless of the amount of activity required. Your focus in setting these milestones is 100% concerned with results. A goal might be making 1,000 sales calls, whereas a milestone is signing your 100th customer regardless of how many sales calls it took to do that. Remember, you get credit only for results in the business world, not unproductive activity. Let the other "busy" companies compete against one another while you focus on achievement.

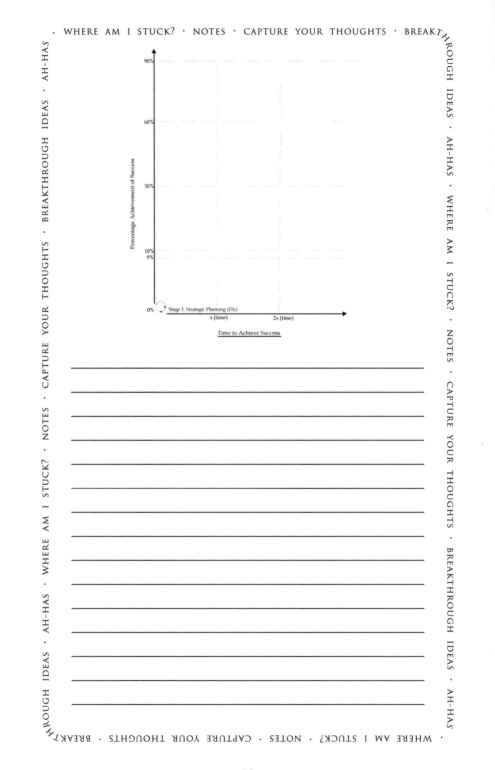

Last, but certainly not least, is your **purpose statement**. The purpose statement answers the questions: What is it about this business that makes me jump out of bed in the morning or burn the candle at both ends at night? Why is your service or product important, and why is your success urgent?

As a business owner, why are you doing this? What is it going to mean to you when you succeed, and who else will benefit from your success when you have reached your milestones and arrived at the future you designed?

Once you've completed this kind of planning, you'll be more certain of where you are going and how to get there. You'll use the power tool of **assessments** on an ongoing basis to help clarify where you are at any given moment. Assessments give you a snapshot of the tangibles and intangibles of your business and all of the people in it. Remember that the personality of the business will mirror the personality of its owner. In turn, the business will mirror the strengths and blind spots of its leadership. Using assessments, you can build on your strengths and protect your blind spots.

During Stage 1, you also want to engage the help of a strategic partner, coach, mentor or advisor. This is someone who will ask you the questions you are not asking yourself and hold you accountable for the commitments that you have made. This person is emotionally invested only in your results, while being casually indifferent to your petty preferences along the way. You'll know you've got the right strategic partner when you find someone who couldn't care less how you feel, but cares deeply whether you succeed or not. Such a person will be skilled in helping you attain your goals.

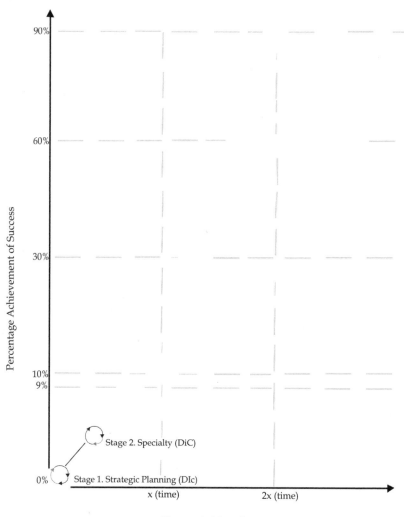

Percentage Achievement of Success

90%

60%

30%

10%
9%

Stage 2. Specialty (DiC)

0%   Stage 1. Strategic Planning (DIc)

x (time)   2x (time)

Time to Achieve Success

STAGE 2:

THE SPECIALTY STAGE

"A Job Is Born"

Y ou've heard that no two snowflakes are alike. Countless trillions fall every snowstorm, but each one is unique. The same is true of human fingerprints, DNA and small businesses. No one possesses the unique set of skills, abilities and experience that you bring to the table with your organization. That powerful truth is what you will begin to utilize in the Specialty Stage. Since your personality is unique, so too will be the personality of your business. You have left Stage 1 and entered Stage 2 because someone has purchased your product or service. Congratulations! You are now trading.

The "big picture" drove you in Stage 1. You needed to create a plan that would inspire you and the marketplace; it is now the passion and energy of you, the owner, that will carry you in Stage 2. In fact, passion along with quality and building your core competence, will be your major focus during this stage. You will also focus, to a lesser degree, on income, although to a lesser degree. Remember that cash keeps you in the game, so you cannot ignore the need to generate sales. Sales will come from your relentless promotion and our infectious enthusiasm for your product or service.

In Stage 2, your blind spot will still be systems. You may often be frustrated because you don't have an effective system to cope with a particular situation. Lack of systems is a functional problem™ of Stage

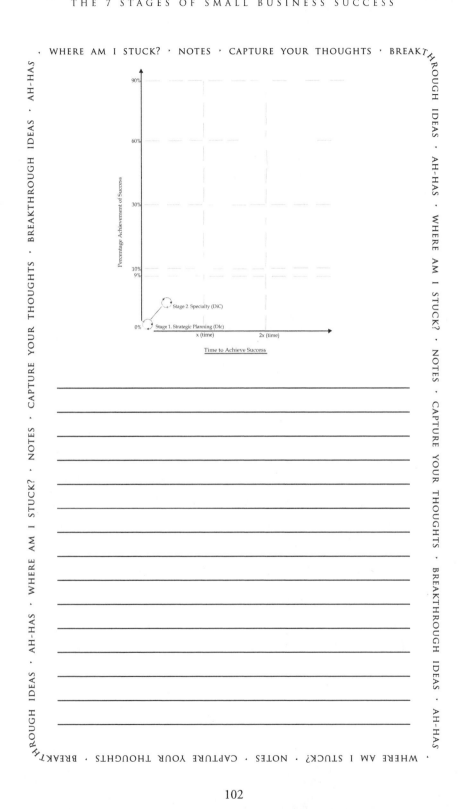

2 businesses. Too many systems would choke the organization before it ever got going. You need the maximum flexibility at this juncture in order to make quick course adjustments as needed. Invoices pile up in a corner; customer calls get routed differently every day. The structure of the company is not in place yet, so this is to be expected. This is simply a functional problem of Stage 2. When it happens (and it will, I promise you) don't panic. Expect it and prepare for it. Customers hire your company because they want YOU at every step of the process. Stage 2 is wonderful because it is a validation that your product, service or idea is a valid and viable one. As Sally Field said when accepting her Academy Award®. "You like me. You really like me!" And your customers like you too. That popularity is the reason that your customers will request you personally for the implementation, the sales calls, the follow ups, the payments, etc. Soon you realize that the business owns you.

Should you choose to address your lack of systems in depth at this time, you will have to move on to Stage 3. If you can make peace with the fact that life will be a bit up in the air for a while, you can maximize Stage 2. In Stage 2, you must capitalize on your expertise.

Your outcome for Stage 2 is to solidify your quality and your core competence. You'll be using 7-Stage Power Tools™ to do this: corporate structuring, advisory board, your DISCoverY Organizational Chart™, your benchmarking, and your branding strategy.

STAGE 2: THE SPECIALTY STAGE

After completing your Strategic Planning from Stage 1, you're on your way to be an MV²P™ organization. The next step is getting that actual

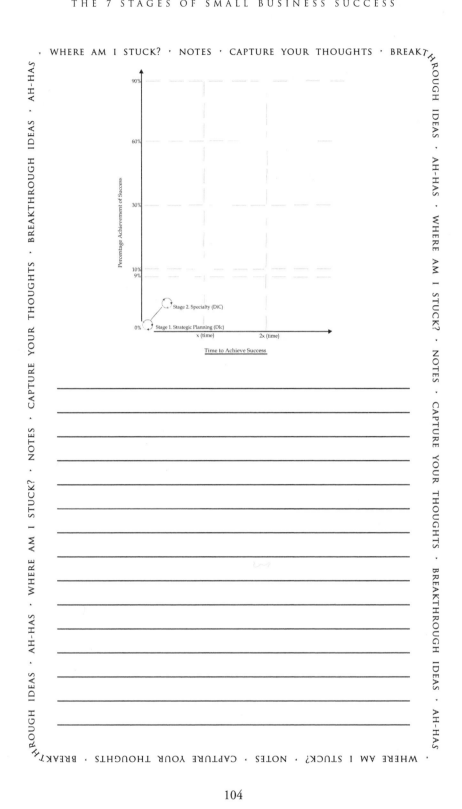

customer: somebody actually purchases your product, service, widget, or idea! Congratulations! You job has just been born. Remember the outcome you are headed for in Stage 2 is to become an expert in your field. Becoming an expert in your field means to obtain the top credentials, top education, top experiences, be part of the top associations in your particular industry. When it comes to your technical expertise, you need to be the smartest person in the room whenever you are called on. What are the highest certifications, accreditations or designations you can receive in your line of work? Is it a PhD, master level, black belt, board-certified? What are the top schools, learning institutions, continuing or higher education facilities? What are the leading professional seminars you can attend? Your credentials don't have to be formal; they can be experiential as well. What experiences do you have that relate to your business? Did you overcome a great obstacle? Have you met or spent time with someone that others normally could not access? Did you complete a significant project, turn around your business, go from rags to riches, scale a tall mountain, lose weight, build muscle, overcome a sickness or injury, invent something, maintain an impressive level of performance, etc.? What trade associations or networking groups do you belong to? What clubs are you part of?

These are just some examples of how you build your professional credentials as an expert in your field. Why is it so important to be an expert in your field? The reality of Stage 2 is that you own a job and not a business. Since there are only so many hours in the day, and only so many billable hours in a month, you need to make sure that you can command the maximum fee for your product or service. A friend's son is in an up-and-coming rock band. I have been to their concerts three times. The audience numbered approximately 200 each time and the ticket cost $10. In the same year I attended a Rolling Stones concert.

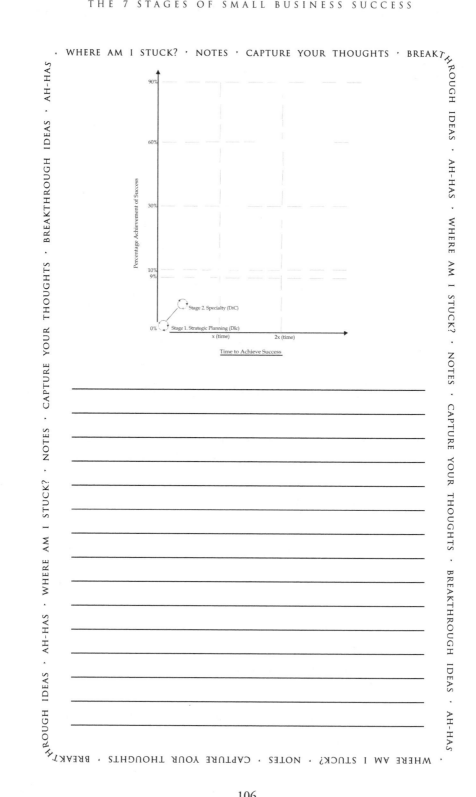

The venue held 77,000 and the ticket was $65. Interestingly, each band played for about the same time, two hours. Two bands, two concerts, two totally separate results. One band generated $2,000 in revenue at the gate, the other $5,005,000 for the same two hours. What is the difference? One band has the credentials; the other does not, yet.

You may have the type of business that will remain a Stage 2 business. Remember that there is no good or bad stage. Being a Stage 2 business has worked extremely well for the Rolling Stones! The crucial take-away from this discussion is that you need to maximize the stage you are in before moving to the next stage.

As you build your core competence, you will develop your brand and image. How are people going to know you? What will they think of when they hear your company name? During Stage 2, you must answer these questions if you are to succeed and maximize Stage 2. Not only do you need to be an expert in your field and achieve the top credentials; you must strive to become among the top *compensated* experts in your field. When you are among the tops, then you know you are ready for Stage 3.

One of the first things to focus on is creating your business identity. What is unique about you? What do you do better than anyone else? Why should someone hire you (or buy from you) over everyone else in your field? We already know that there is no one else like you in the world. You are the best in the world at being you. That's the good news. Your unique attributes and skills let you know what you do best. Build your business on your core strengths by embracing who you are when you're at your best. Your company SHOULD reflect your individual personality at this stage. Let who you are radiate and shine through for all to see. Richard Branson is cheeky and irreverent. Those traits

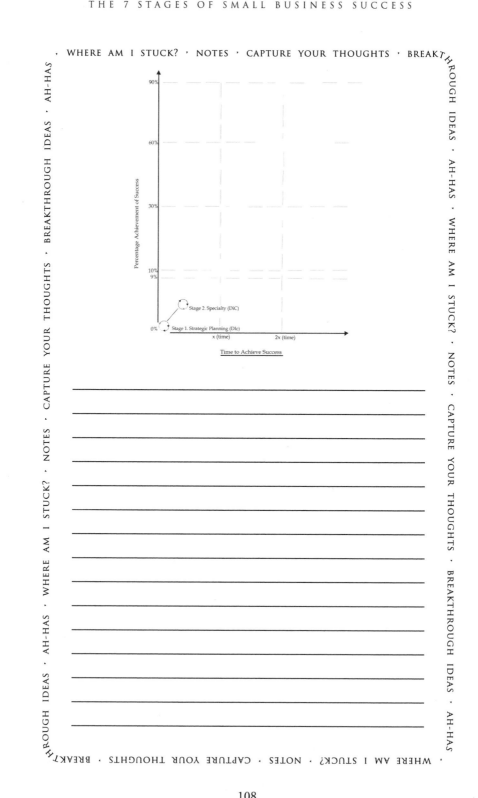

have become symbolic of his Virgin Companies. He has perfected that irreverence to the point that he has grown into a Stage 5 business and a greater than billion-pound personal net worth. More than 200 independently owned companies carry the Virgin label.

There is a local ice cream shop where I live that makes the best soft ice cream cones. From March to October people wait in line for the best ice cream cone around. Years ago, I had a landscape design and installation company. I offered a money-back guarantee on the shrubs and trees I planted even though I was not the one who would care for them. My customers could abuse the plantings for up to one year and still be eligible for a replacement. I had a competitive advantage over my competitors in my area and had very few replacement claims. My favorite Italian restaurant makes homemade lasagna that is to die for. You can't get it anywhere else. Once they altered the recipe for variety, but there was such an outcry from the patrons that they returned to the original recipe and haven't changed it in 20 years. Same dish, same owner, same servers, same bar manager, same great experience. Result? A loyal customer base that fills that restaurant seven days per week. What is your competitive advantage? What do you do or offer that is unique in your market?

Perfect what you're already good at and you'll build your core competence. Become an expert in your chosen field. It isn't always easy, but the payoff is immense.

You'll notice that in our Personal DISCoverY Wheel™, you can design from the inside out so you can build on your strengths. Live your truth. Be yourself and make no apologies for it. The entrepreneurial spirit in you may not have been reinforced positively in school or as a child growing up. You were probably louder, talked more, had

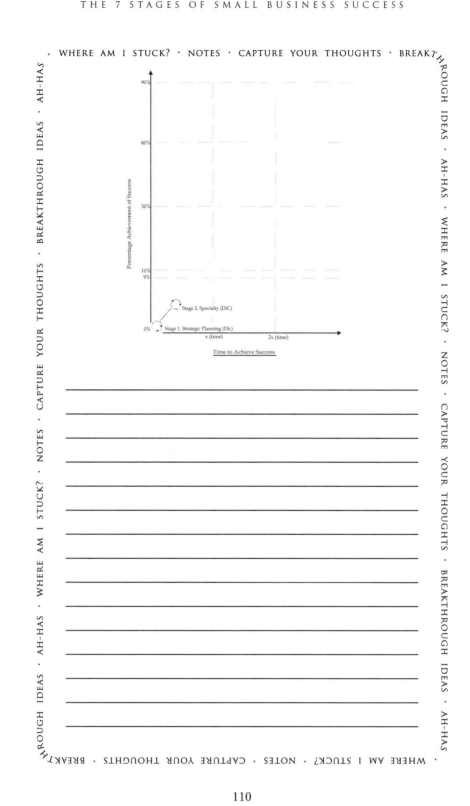

Stage 2. Specialty (DiC)

Stage 1. Strategic Planning (DIc)

Time to Achieve Success

_____
_____
_____
_____
_____
_____
_____
_____
_____
_____
_____
_____
_____
_____
_____

boundless energy. You questioned authority. You made suggestions and asked a lot of questions. Since you were good at many things, you may have been teased. Your life was mostly about compliance, learning the rules of the game, and getting things right. You were rewarded for your answers in school. Now, you will be rewarded for the questions you ask. Business ownership is your opportunity to shine. The more you are true to yourself and your vision of what gift you were born to share with the world, the better the chance that you will ultimately succeed.

You want to build the quality of your product or service early in Stage 2, which means continuously developing those credentials. If you work at this, you will find that your brand will begin to gain momentum in your sales toward the middle of this stage. If you own a sandwich shop, make the best sandwich in town. Word will get out and you will attract more customers. That's when you'll see those testimonials start coming in and gain endorsements and loyalty to your product. All the time you do, you'll continue to hone the quality of your product. That's going to be your focus. Most businesses live in this stage for the majority of the their life. In Stage 2, you have the most control over every area of the business. Since BOEs feel that no one can do things as good as they can, they often stay in Stage 2. There is a comfort zone with this stage that does not exist in any other stage. Moving into Stage 3 requires a BOE to create policies and procedures, delegate to others, play nice in the sandbox, and exercise patience. These are not the normal strengths of BOEs; they are the very things that BOEs fled from in past work environments. Most sole proprietorships, micro, small and medium-size businesses spend the more time in Stage 2 than all of the other stages *combined.*.

What does it mean to be an expert in a field? Elvis Presley and The Beatles didn't invent music, but they innovated in ways that catapulted

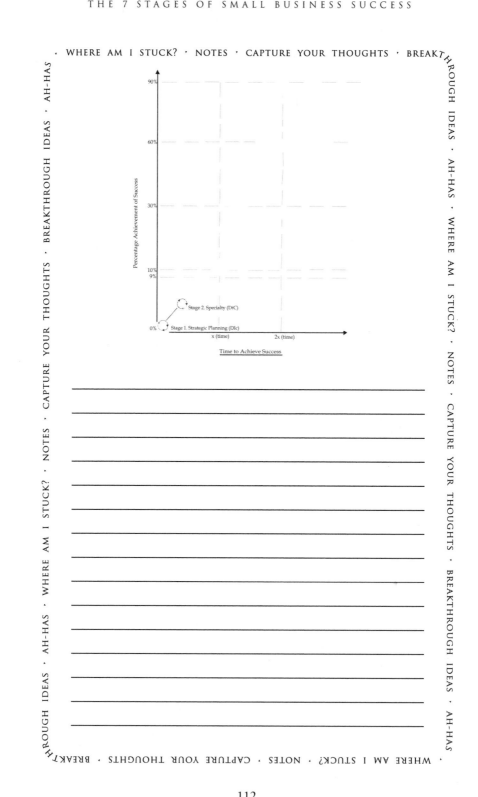

them to the top of the industry. Many professions have a clearly marked path to mastery. Doctors and surgeons go through medical school, internship, residency and specialization training. Even then they aren't allowed to practice until they become board-certified. I don't know about you, but I'm glad they have to gain all that experience before they cut me open!

Do you know what they call the student who graduates from medical school with extremely high grades? They call him "Doctor." Do you know what they call the student who graduates in the same class from the same medical school with poor grades? They call him "Doctor" also. Who do you want cutting you open? The consumer wants you to have the top credentials. The consumer will pay more for your product or service if you obtain the top credentials. You owe it to your customers to give them the best of you.

You may need to chart your own path to mastery in your business. Seek out the highest level of credentials available. Learn all you can about how to perfect your product or service. Read trade publications, attend conferences, and gain as much exposure as possible to as many high level people in the industry.

During Stage 2, the business tends to run the owner. You are more self-employed than a business owner. The government would technically define you as a business entity. In all practicality, you are self-employed. You own a job. The business owns that job. In many ways, the business owns you. This is no small concern, which is why you need to devote serious time to implementing your MV²P Planning™.

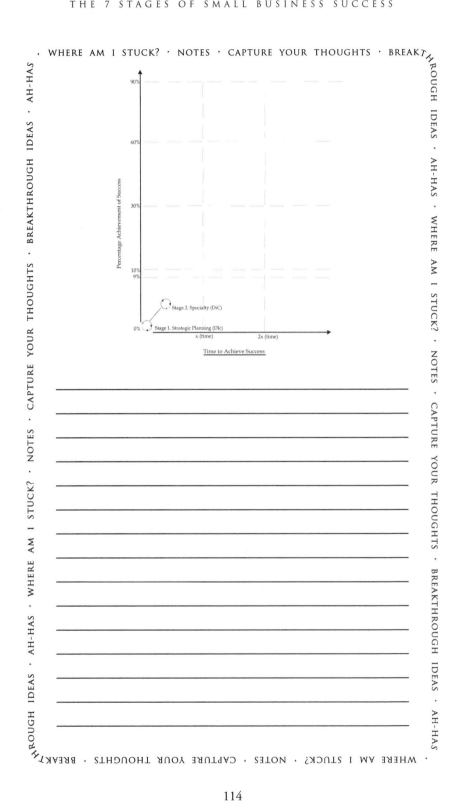

Percentage Achievement of Success

90%

60%

30%

10%
9%

Stage 2. Specialty (DiC)

0%   Stage 1. Strategic Planning (DIc)
     x (time)   2x (time)

Time to Achieve Success

_____

_____

_____

_____

_____

_____

_____

_____

_____

_____

_____

_____

_____

_____

_____

This means working with your strategic advisor to implement your plans while building your industry-specific credentials. The need for a strategic advisor is crucial in Stage 2. The fastest way to grow your business is to know when you are on track with your plan and that you are getting it right. You want to minimize course adjustments. The closer you remain to the successful execution of your MV^{2}P^{TM} plan, the faster you reach ultimate success. As an owner, it is very clear when you get something wrong. There is usually immediate feedback with a consequence attached to it. Change your hours of operation and fewer people show up, you got it wrong. Change your recipe and there is an uproar, you got it wrong. How do you know when you have gotten right? Is it always clear? The leaders in every industry use a team of strategic advisors to help them increase their skill implement their plan *and let them know when they are on the right track.* Remember that it is the little things that make the master. There is a very small margin between the top performers and the middle performers. A CBS golf telecast in 2001 displayed a fascinating statistic. Tiger Woods, then the Number 1- ranked golfer in the world, had an average score of 69.12 per round of golf. Quite impressive. What was even more interesting is that the second- (Phil Mickelson) and third-ranked (Ernie Els) golfers had average scores of 69.23 and 69.54, respectively. The margin between Tiger Woods and the nearest competitor was approximately *one-tenth of a stroke* over the four rounds of the tournament. Even though their scores were close, were their results close? Absolutely not. Mastery in your field is at your fingertips. There is little that separates you from the very best in your field! Roger Staubach, a professional football legend and successful entrepreneur, once said that there is not much traffic on the extra mile. It is the little things that make the master. You will maximize Stage 2 by making sure you are among the most highly credentialed and compensated in your field.

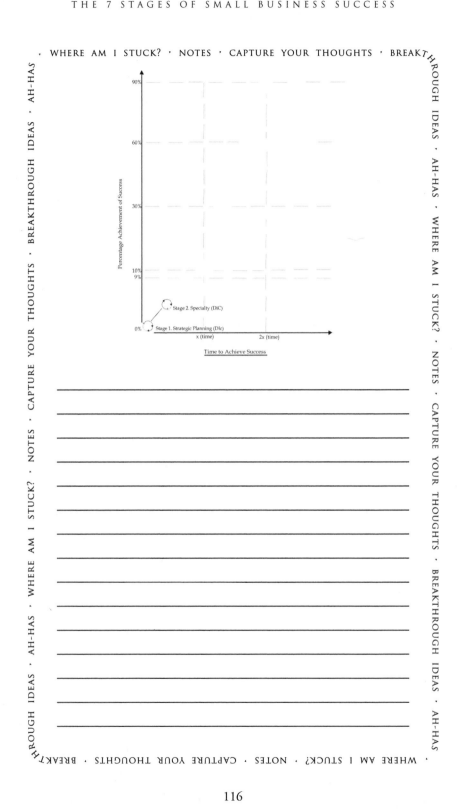

Since you are still doing a great deal of the work yourself, there is a limit to what you can earn. There are only so many hours in the day, and whether you're a tradesman, doctor, financial planner, accountant or an attorney, there is a limit to the number of clients you can service yourself. Part of your strategy for establishing your company is ensuring that you are among the top-paid in your field. This is crucial to establishing your expertise. You must take both of these realities into account when you are setting fees and allocating your time and effort. Your brand and the perceived quality of your product or service will ultimately be judged by the price you charge. The more you charge, the more perceived quality. The less you charge, the less the perceived quality. Consumer Reports magazine ranks the automobile industry in many categories, including quality, reliability, and the number of reported repairs per 1,000 cars manufactured. By and large, the most expensive cars are manufactured in Europe. The also happen to be among the most prestigious brands. By and large the most economically priced cars are manufactured in Asia. Even though they are the most expensive and the quality is perceived to be the highest, European brands tend to have the most problems per 1,000, and the number of problems outpace their competitors' as the cars age. Asian cars tend to be the most reliable, best-performing, and have the least problems per 1,000 when new and as they age. Yet we still continue to aspire to purchase those high-priced brands, considering them to be high status symbols. Building a premium brand is about charging a high fee, and then adding features and accessories to your product or service to justify that higher fee.

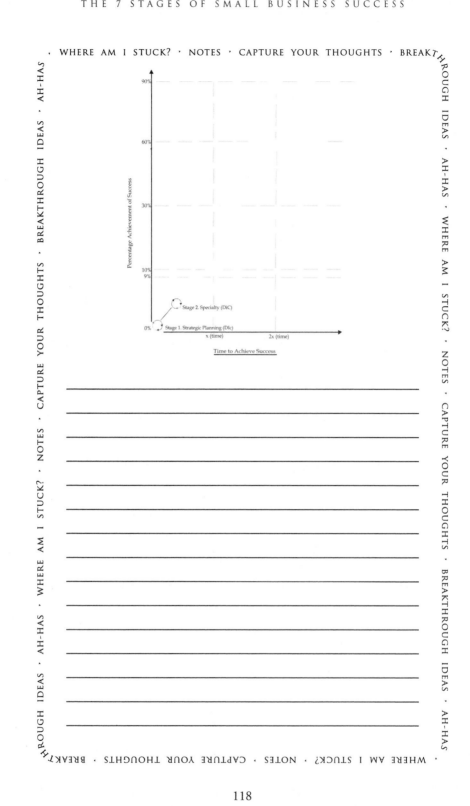

Percentage Achievement of Success

90%

60%

30%

10%
9%

Stage 2. Specialty (DiC)

0% Stage 1. Strategic Planning (DIc)

x (time)   2x (time)

Time to Achieve Success

_____

_____

_____

_____

_____

_____

_____

_____

_____

_____

_____

_____

_____

POWER TOOLS FOR STAGE 2

The first Power Tool you will use in Stage 2 is the creation of your **advisory board**: Who are the other professionals and experts you want around you? You will need an attorney and a legal advisor. You will need an accountant and a tax advisor. Of course your attorney and legal advisor could be the same person and your accountant might do your taxes. On the other hand, you might decide that you need a tax advisor who plays a greater strategic role in larger decisions. This might mean you select someone with broader experience who won't be actually filing the paperwork for your company.

Your advisory board also needs someone who understands business valuation and someone who is a financial benchmarking expert. You want to make sure that you have your strategic partner in place: that coach, advisor or mentor. This is the individual who serves as a sounding board for your ideas but also possesses the skill of facilitation. He or she will actually facilitate the meetings when you bring your strategic advisors together. Once you produce the agenda, it is actually counter-productive for you to facilitate that meeting. You as the owner are "in the picture," so you can't see the whole picture. During your meetings, you will need a facilitator to be the "bad cop." When an unpopular decision or comment is to be made, that will be the job of the facilitator. You need an advisor who can see the whole picture in order to effectively manage the meeting and achieve the desired outcome of having all of the voices and opinions heard so that the owner can make the most educated and informed decision for the business. You need to remain the "good cop" so others feel free to share their opinions, no matter how good or ridiculous they may be. The Hall of Fame baseball player Cal Ripken Jr. was well-known and beloved for the extra time he would devote to his fans. After each home game, Cal would sign auto-

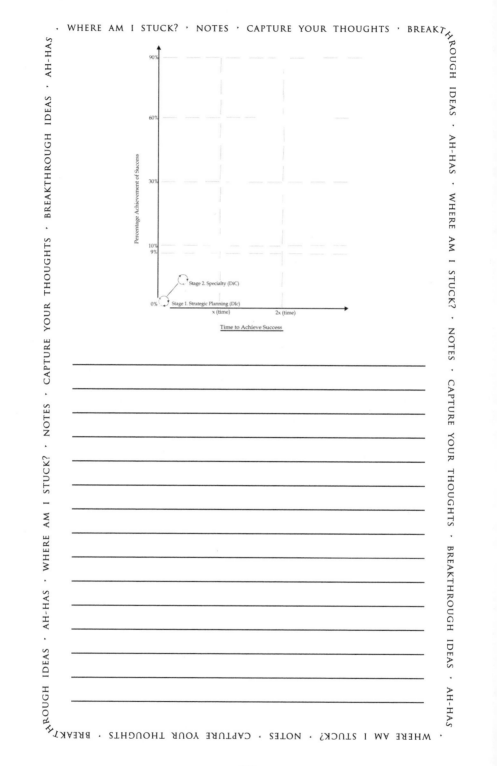

graphs well after most of the other ballplayers had left the stadium. He always employed someone from his organization to be his "bad cop." At some point, the autograph signing had to stop. Invariably there was some kid who waited on line who was going to be disappointed and not receive an autograph. Cal could not be seen as the bad cop. He would shake his pen as if to signify that the pen was running out of ink. That was the cue for his bad cop to step in and let the crowd know that Mr. Ripken had to go inside and end the autograph signing session. Cal would of course play the role of good cop, roll his shoulder in an "aw-shucks" fashion and then smile and wave to the crowd, thanking them for coming and hoping they would come again (which of course they did). For a list of "bad cops," go to www.the7stages.com/badcops.

You need an advisor who can see the whole picture in order to effectively manage the meeting and allow all of the voices and opinions to be heard so that you can make the most educated and informed decision for the business. So it is very important to have someone with those skills on your board.

The next Power Tool you'll be utilizing is **Corporate Structuring**. That is, creating your DISCoverY Organizational Chart™. This can be understood as splitting the business in two. What business functions bring cash and customers in (customers and sales)? What business functions keep them in (delivers the products or service, fulfills the customer order; and makes sure that the details are handled impeccably to insure top quality)? List all those tasks and their descriptions along with the names of the individuals assigned to each.

Your unique selling proposition guides you in your branding strategy. How are you going to become distinct in your industry and eventually lead it? What is your Unique Client Experience™? How are you

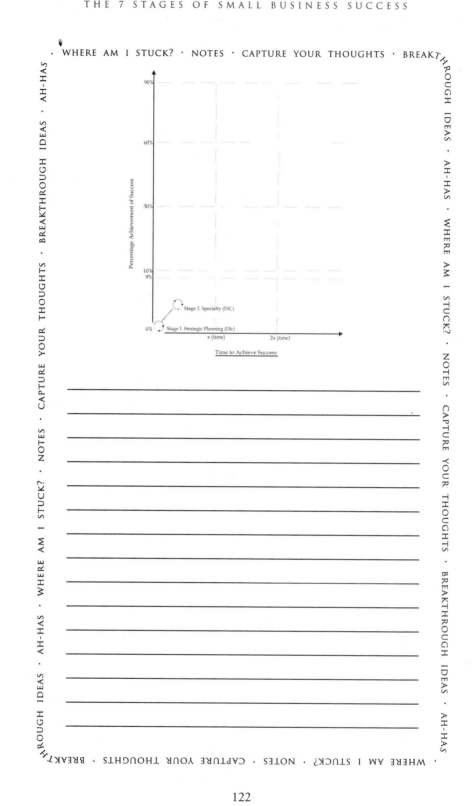

_____
_____
_____
_____
_____
_____
_____
_____
_____
_____
_____
_____
_____
_____

going to create an experience for your client that is different from what anyone else can offer? Starbucks felt that their clients were not receiving the optimum experience that they had in the past. So the company took radical action. On February 26, 2008, Starbucks closed all of its 7,100 locations for three hours to retrain employees on the Starbucks experience. Without the experience that is unique to its locations and brand, Starbucks would be just another coffee bean. Remember that your product or service is a commodity. *The relationship that you create with your customers is priceless and timeless.* A top restaurant sells not only great food but also a great atmosphere. You will be deciding what that atmosphere or experience will be for your clients and how you will achieve it.

As you've determined what is unique about your company, you've also created a number of targets and objectives for the branding process. Your next task is to discover how the work you have done so far measures up to the optimum standard in your field. You will also evaluate the performance of each individual and team within your business with the same criteria. That means it is time for an exercise called DISCoverY **Benchmarking**.

Benchmarking articulates key achievements for the tangibles and intangibles of a business. The tangibles are the numbers: the 28% of the value of your business that's based on the revenues, costs of goods sold, gross profit, net profit, and other measurable quantities. When you benchmark, you compare your performance in each and every line of your financial statements against the industry average. The results of your DISCoverY Diagnostics gives you clear targets to aim for in order to outperform and eventually eliminate your competition. When you benchmark, you determine the industry averages in each of the areas of your financial statements. You need to know what you're up

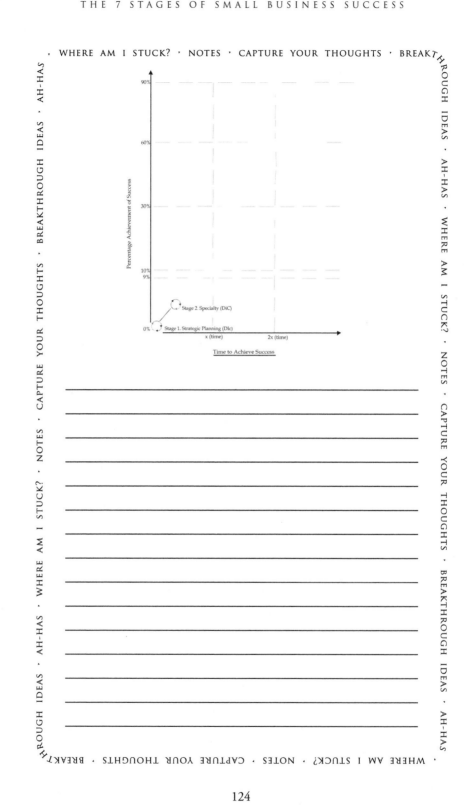

against. Who is your competition and what are they up to? You have to understand the competition before you can eliminate it. This analysis will allow you to determine how you compare with everyone else in the industry, as well as giving you a clear target for the current stage. After this exercise you will know what it takes to become Number 1 in your industry, whether that's your goal or not. To learn more about benchmarking and the DISCoverY Diagnostics™ go to www.the7stages.com/assessments.

Your business' intangibles are the human component. You don't benchmark the people themselves, you benchmark their positions and the roles they play in the business. This means you create the prototype for each position. You go back to your DISCoverY Organizational Chart™, where you have your salespeople, marketing team, assistants, secretary, accountants, bookkeepers and receptionists. Then you benchmark each job in the business. What is the ideal standard for that particular position? In his book *Good to Great*, Jim Collins uses a great analogy for making sure you hire the correct people. Pretend that your business is a bus. You want to get the wrong people off of the bus, get the right people on the bus, and get them in the right seats before you pull away. What the author is describing is selection. Just as every individual has a personality, so too does every job. You need to make sure that the person is right for the job. For a salesperson, you want someone who is outgoing, optimistic, enthusiastic, persuasive; a promoter at heart. For someone in administration or operations, you want someone who is stable, scheduled, systematic, predicable and reliable; a team player. For someone in bookkeeping, accounting, legal or finance, you want some who is meticulous, conservative, detail-oriented, organized and precise; a perfectionist. Your employees' true natures must harmonize with the needs of their jobs so they will produce outstanding results.

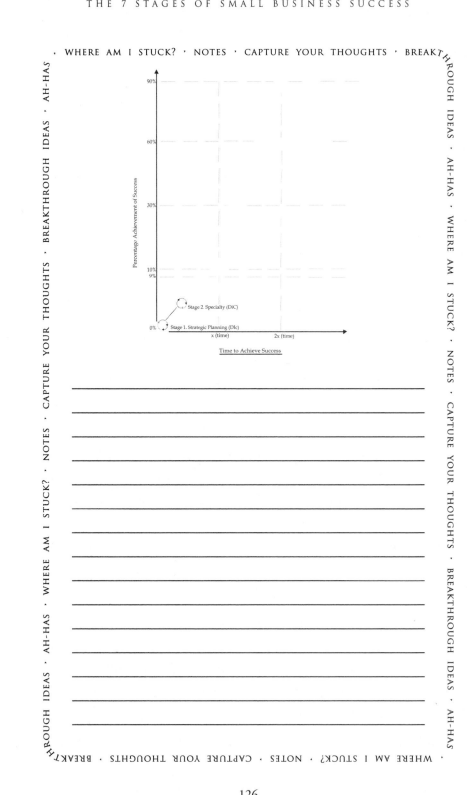

If not, the job and the performance of the company will suffer. While there will be similarities in these positions from company to company, your business is unique. Every position will be unique and the top performer will meet a unique set of standards.

Once you have benchmarked every individual position, you compare those benchmarks with the assessments of you and your employees in Stage 1. Then, you grow and coach those people to perform at the benchmark levels for their positions. Want to be the best? Create the prototype and then work toward it. A client of mine wanted to hire an executive assistant. We went through a process that determined what tasks (s)he would perform, roles and responsibilities, hours expected to work, etc. Once we determined the job description, we then profiled the 'ultimate employee', the prototype. We considered the preferred behavioral style, values hierarchy, required personal attributes that would be the best fit for the position. Once we 'benchmarked the position' (by the way, you don't don't benchmark people, you benchmark positions. You coach and guide people to empowerment, self-awareness and ultimately, the highest possible levels of productivity). Once the position was clearly defined, we used the descriptor words and phrases in the advertisements to attract the best qualified candidates. Using these assessment tools, along with the candidate resume and interview, we were able to identify and hire someone who was a very close match to the benchmark! Is this a perfect and exact science? Of course not. You will, however, give yourself the best chance for success when using this approach. Once we found the most qualified candidate, we then coached that person to achieve their fullest potential. The result? The right person was in the right role doing the right job happily and productively each day.

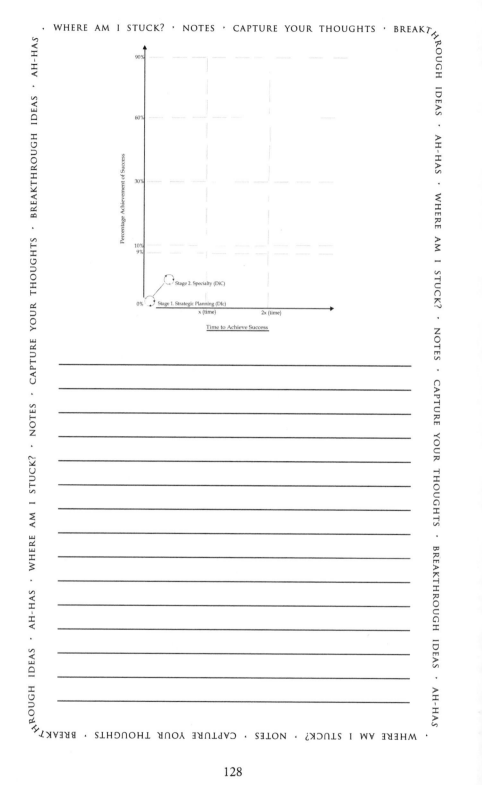

To learn how to benchmark a position and then hire, develop and train your employees to achieve and maintain that standard, please go to www.the7stages.com/assessments.

This process of benchmarking is an aspect of the 7-Stage process that will give you a competitive advantage over everyone else in your industry. Your ability to assess the teams as functional units and benchmark the entire company on the intangible side helps you make tactical adjustments on a regular basis. This keeps you constantly moving toward your goals and milestones.

Assessing the team forces you to get into a little more detail, and there is a 7-Stage technology that will assist in that process. To understand where your business will go as a unit, you need to understand not only how your employees work as individuals but also how to maximize them as a team. In the 7-Stage methodology we provide a framework that allows you to understand how a group should function optimally as a team.

STRENGTHENING YOUR CORE

By assessing the people and benchmarking the positions, you are effectively growing your organization from the inside out. You are strengthening your core competency, which is the major focus of Stage 2. This is why we call it the *Specialty Stage*. You are a specialist. You need to be the best. If your widget represents a great concept, but falls apart after three months, you're not going to build a loyal clientele. If your service leaves something to be desired, it probably won't matter whether your rates undercut the competition.

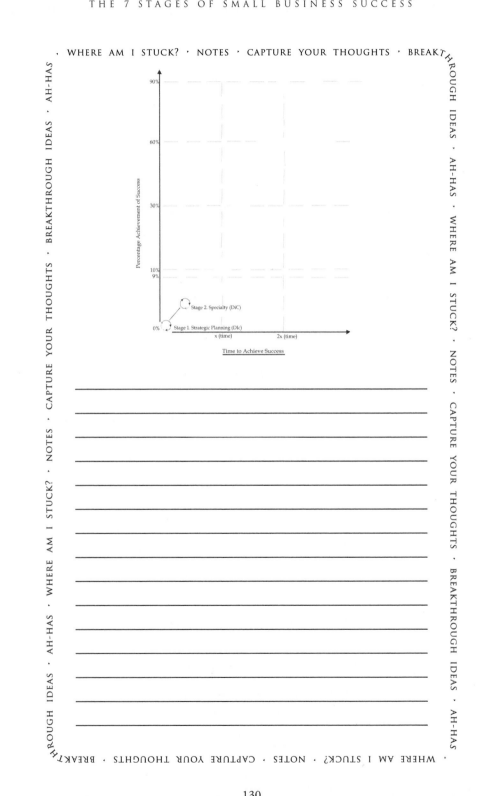

To be the best, you strengthen from the core. You strengthen your numbers, people, teams, and organization from the inside. You learn what it takes to reach the top of your industry, and you utilize your Power Tools to take you there.

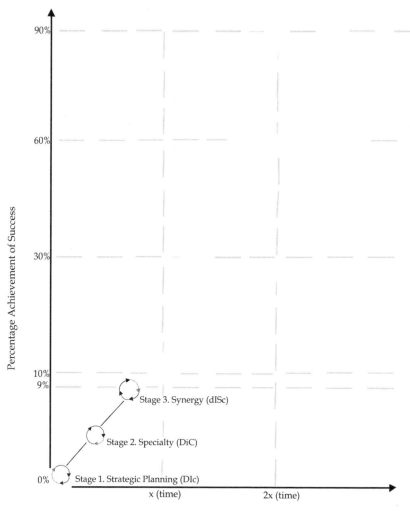

STAGE 3:

THE SYNERGY STAGE

"A Sandbox Is Born!"

Renowned speaker and psychologist Connie Podesta once quipped, "Life would be so much easier if weren't for other people." The Synergy Stage is your attempt to develop and nurture the strategic relationships that will help your enterprise bridge the gap between self-employment specialist (where you own your job; and the job owns you); and running a systematized business that will run itself. No one person is all things to all people. However, your business MUST be all things to its customers or you risk losing them to another company that can provide your product or service better, faster or cheaper. In other words, your business must have an inspiring vision, robust sales and marketing, effective and efficient systems, and watertight controls with meticulous attention to detail.

In Stage 3 you are going to build the type of relationships with partners, subcontractors, affiliates, and key employees that will help you grow the business. You will develop synergy with key people who will take on more responsibility and will guide the company at a strategic level. In Stage 3, you will complete your dream team of advisors.

The Number 1 personal virtue that will be tested at this point is your patience. You will need to be patient with *yourself.* You can't do it all. You need to accept that you need help in order to get to the promised land. Further, you need to *embrace* the fact that you will need to leverage

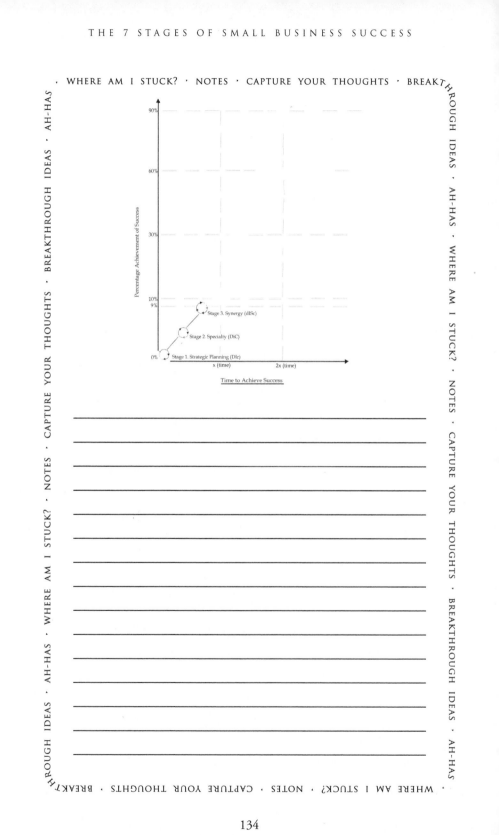

Percentage Achievement of Success

90%

60%

30%

10%
9%

Stage 3. Synergy (dISc)

Stage 2. Specialty (DiC)

0%

Stage 1. Strategic Planning (DIc)

x (time)

2x (time)

Time to Achieve Success

other people and their talents in order to achieve the vision you have for your business. Your business, in order to reach its ultimate potential and level of success, must be all things to its customers. You must begin to build a team that can contribute to the growth of the business at a very high level; making "big picture" recommendations and decisions. These key employees and advisors should not be yes-men. They should challenge you, give you feedback, and contradict you for the sake and betterment of the company. In Stage 2, you were self-employed. If your goal is to grow a business that can function on its own, you must move into Stage 3

This is the first stage where you must give significant attention to all four components of your business: direction, income, structure and controls.

1. Direction (D) – The big-picture planning of your business. Designing your business (on paper). Your vision and mission must be so compelling that it inspires and motivates others to join in your crusade.

2. Income (I) - The sales and marketing function of your business. This part of the business generates new customers and upselling opportunities to existing customers (marketing). Once these leads are generated, you then sell and close the deal (sales). This is the relationship building and the Unique Client Experience or UCE™ that you design and nurture with your external customers.

3. Systems (S) - The day-to-day operations that are needed to run the business. These operations fall in two basic categories. **First, what needs to be done on a daily basis even if no customers call on you today?** For example, who sorts the mail, who answers the e-mails, who turns the lights and the machinery on at the beginning of the shift and

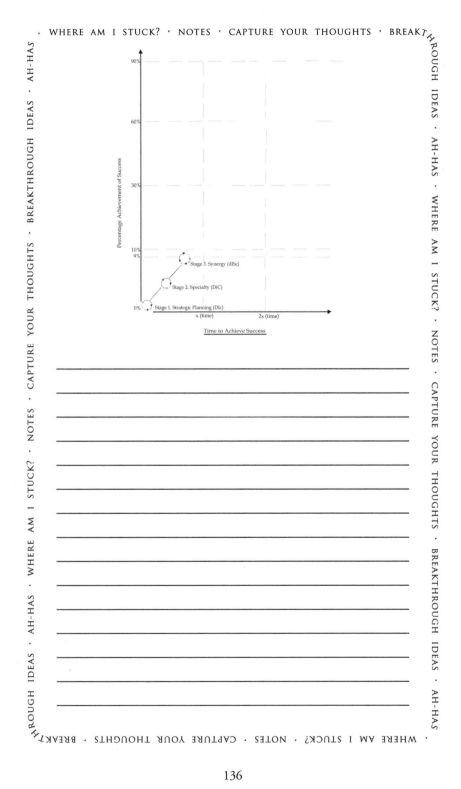

off at the end? Who pays the bills and when? Who receives and sign for deliveries? Who makes the deposits at the bank? Who cleans up the office and removes the trash? Who services the machinery and vehicles? Who organizes the receipts? Who prepares and files the taxes? **Second, what needs to be done on a daily basis when customers call on you today?** Who answers the phones? Who staffs the reception desk? Who follows up with clients? Who addresses customer needs? Who manufactures the product, and how? Who packs and ships? Who delivers it?

4. Controls (C). The controls are the details. What checks and balance do you have in place to make sure that you don't make mistakes and that you get tasks right the first time? Controls make sure that you keep as much as (legally) possible from what you earn. Checks and balances mean that you have the proper insurance coverage, contracts that protect you and your intellectual property, a good credit report, etc. Attention to the small things will make a huge impact in your business. What feature of your product, service or idea makes you unique and gives you a competitive advantage. What SMALL distinction will make a BIG difference? The heaven is in the detail. These four components require constant attention and would overwhelm even the sharpest of entrepreneurs. You need to build a team whose strength is in each of the four components of the business.

But your major focus will be creating structure. This is vital for the long-term success of your business. At the same time, you will still need to invest time planning, moving your vision forward, and maintaining high levels of quality. The graph on www.the7stages.com/graph shows the major emphasis of Stage 3 in the I area, which is income and interaction. The S area during this particular stage denotes structure. All the while, you cannot neglect your MV²P Planning™ or your quality. You can see why Stage 3 is the graveyard for most small businesses.

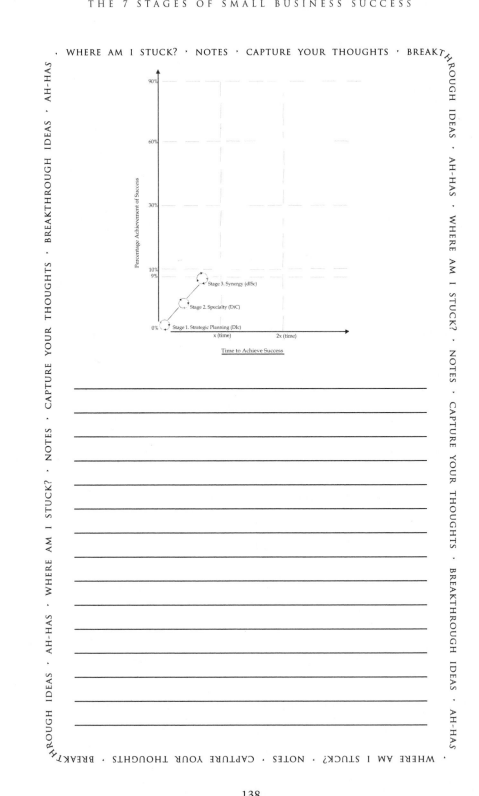

So how do you make sure that your dream doesn't get a tombstone and an epitaph in the Synergy Stage? You take a good look at your Stage 3 blind spot: patience and self-management. *You need to be patient with yourself.* This stage will bring it all to the surface: the areas in which you may not have performed to your standard and the areas where you flat-out failed. You might start to see a recurrence of issues that caused the demise of a past enterprise. You may even begin to feel the dream slipping away.

Don't worry. This isn't a life cycle, where every strategy is just another ploy to cheat death for a while. This is the Success Cycle™: You can stop anytime and reverse course. You can become younger, faster and newer. Whether you're a new business on the way up or you're an existing business rebranding, you can turn it around. And you can do that right here in Stage 3.

Give yourself a break. Your "weaknesses" are not permanent qualities; they are areas for growth and improvement. They are, ultimately, strengths in development. You don't need to continuously beat yourself up if your filing system is inefficient. Research new software, talk to your advisor, and relax. Focus 10% of your energy on identifying the challenge and the other 90% of your energy on the solution.

CHALLENGES WITH NET PROFIT

There are many functional challenges at this stage as well. While cash flow should not be a problem, profit may still present a challenge. Poor cash flow at this stage would indicate a dysfunction. If you maximized Stage 2 and became an expert in your field, then you are a specialist who is at the top of the field and you're bringing in a lot of money.

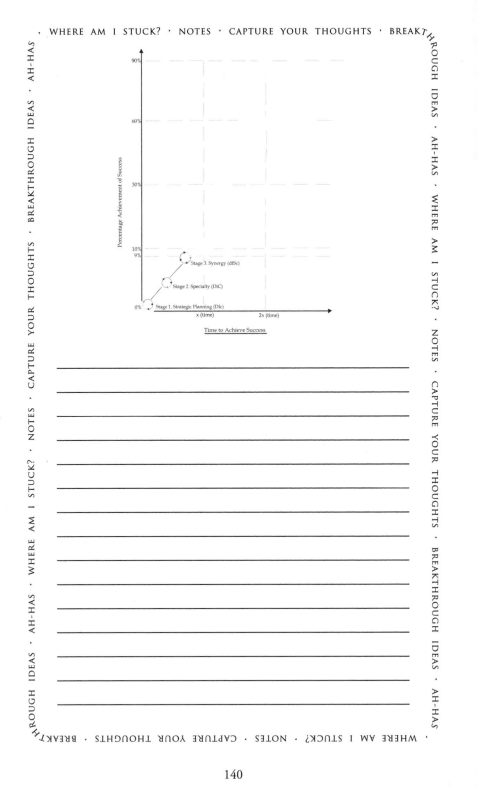

In Stage 3, you're putting corporate structure in place, so you are still reinvesting a great deal of money into your business. Building structure means building a team. (See the DISCoverY Organizational Chart™). Although you're generating plenty of business and earning a lot of income, this reinvestment in structure means your expenses will be a little high. Although this may feel frustrating, it is the price you must pay for the long-term success of your company. Patience. You will be rewarded exponentially in Stages 4-7 for the work you do in Stage 3.

Your net profit will be a little lower while creating and developing your team. During Stage 2, you defined and benchmarked those positions and assessed the people. Now you are putting the structure in place and starting to plug those people into that structure. To paraphrase Jim Collins, in *Good to Great*: Get the wrong people off the bus, get the right people ON the bus, and then get them in the right seats.

SYSTEMS AT LAST

Our outcome for the Synergy Stage is to train the team members in their core competence, making them the best they can be. At the end of Stage 3, you will have defined and refined your structure. You created your job descriptions in Stage 1; now you will draw upon all your experiences in the first two stages to create your policy and procedure manuals.

You're also about to cover the area that has been your blind spot thus far: systems. You are identifying and designing those systems now so you can create and implement them in the next stage. At this point, it becomes crucial to delegate some of your day-to-day tasks to others so that you can focus on building and refining that structure.

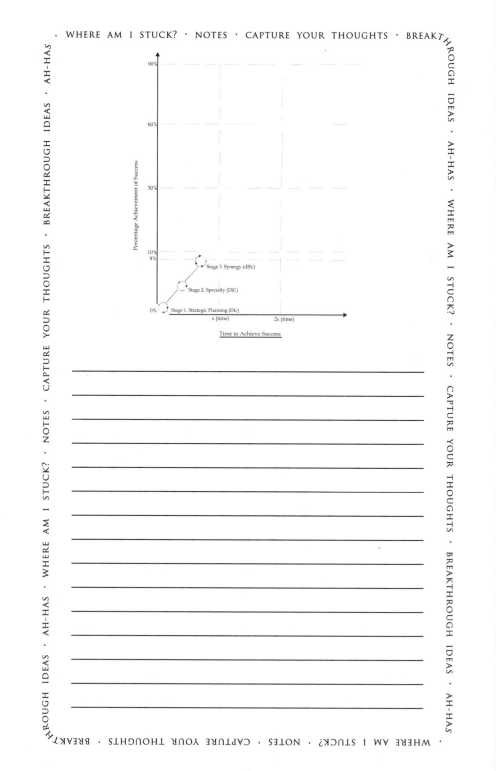

Remember the rules of the sandbox: Play nice with others! You need to create a partnership with your employees. They are your internal customers. Make sure their experiences with you make them want to be a long-term part of the vision.

Stage 3 is full of intangibles, such as intellectual property, processes, branding – and mostly the people and their performance. In 21st-century entrepreneurship, your people and their performance drive the value in your business. This dynamic is the reason it is essential that you play nice in the sandbox and select an aligned and inspired team. This is a stage of people and communication. You've made your plans, perfected your product, and now you are training the people who will take you to seven figures.

Your goal is to make working for you as simple as possible by clearly defining their roles and writing concise and comprehensible policy and procedure manuals. You want your employees to put their energy into their work, not into figuring out what you want or what is expected of them. You also troubleshoot on an ongoing basis, which allows them to refine and redefine their roles. You respond by refining your policies, making sure that you leave no stone unturned. This is the process whereby you begin to develop and articulate what will become the systems of your business in the next stage.

Once your manuals are complete, you must empower your employees to do their jobs. You need to let them go. In a way, you become their strategic partner by enabling them to take the initiative to complete their tasks. The sales representatives are free to work with *their* clients; administrators are empowered to run *their* office, and so on.

Resisting the temptation to micromanage is central to your success for the remainder of the stages. You need to create a safe space for your

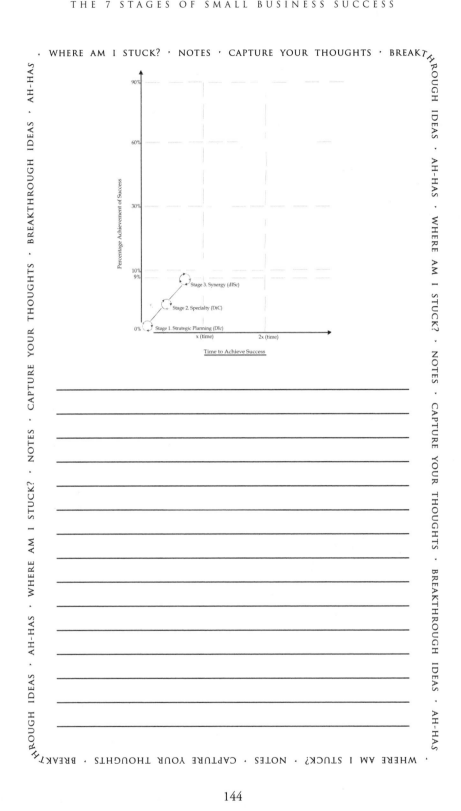

_____

_____

_____

_____

_____

_____

_____

_____

_____

_____

_____

_____

employees to take initiative and sometimes to get it wrong. Everyone will make mistakes or execute poorly at times. Remember that people learn from their successes and failures and you need to allow them to do both. They must also feel safe to succeed. This culture is important, because as you have followed the recommendations in Stage 1 and 2, you will notice an interesting dynamic developing. It will unearth one of your deepest fears: that you have invested all of this time energy and capital in these people and they will not do the job as well as you can. I can tell you now, that you will be correct. They will not do the job as well as you. **They will do the job much better than you ever could have or ever dreamed!** You must wrap your arms (and head) around the idea that as you follow the recommendations in this book, your employees may surpass your performance level in the areas in which you were not proficient. They will surpass you because it is in their true nature to do that job and they will naturally and effortlessly excel at it.

Your strategic partners are the Power Tool for the Synergy Stage and your coach, mentor and advisor. You will be leaning heavily on their advice and expertise. You'll also need to give significant effort to managing yourself. What does this mean? Practically speaking, self-management is your ability to set and keep your commitments. It means you can say no to a sale or say no to a poor customer. It means you go home at 5 p.m. when you say you're going to go home. When you're managing yourself, you bite your tongue when you know can do a job faster and better than an employee. This will be a counter-intuitive skill, since you got where you are today by taking risks and saying yes when the whole world said no. That's why you need your strategic partners: a neutral third party to work with you.

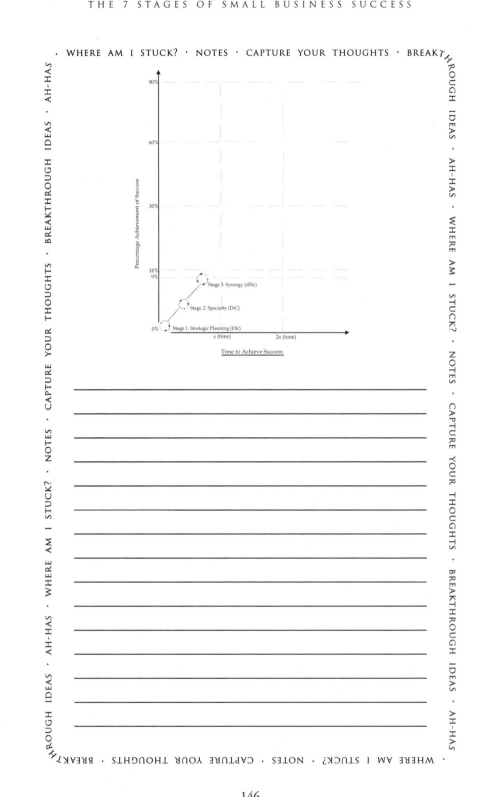

TRAINING, TRAINING, TRAINING

This is the internal training stage. The goal of your training is to create an alignment that will prepare your team, employees and executives for the future. The higher a building, the deeper and more secure its foundation must be. Your training efforts in Stage 3 will determine the heights to which your company can soar in the future. The Cornell study found one-third of employees are not right for their jobs, one-third are not right for their companies, and one-half are not prepared for the future. Your Stage 3 training will address those realities.

The hallmark of Stage 3 is Continuous Professional Development (CPD). Don't hold back with this: Train everybody on your staff, even the ones who you think are not going to stay. It's very tempting to neglect those you would consider firing. But your training may effectively address their blind spots or redefine their roles in such a way that they become ideal employees. You can only identify diamonds in the rough after you polish them off. CPD polishes them and allows them to excel if they have the desire.

It is much cheaper, more effective and efficient to equip existing employees in the area of their core competency than to hire new people. Before you let anyone go, you need to make sure that you gave that employee every opportunity to be successful in the business. This means implementing CPD proactively, instead of waiting for catastrophic problems. Again, this will be a lot easier if you anticipate the need to invest in this area during this stage.

Remember that this stage will make or break your future: In some respects you will feel as if you are in crisis mode a lot of the time. Everything is happening at once and you barely have time to catch your breath. You've done your MV²P Planning™ and allocated your

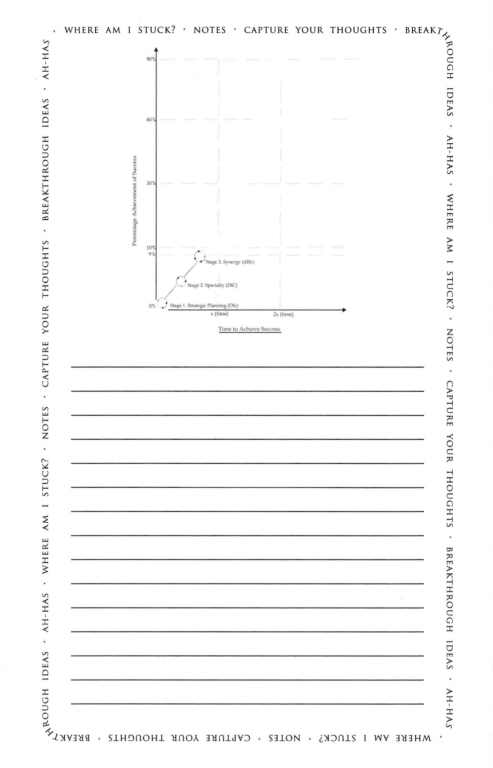

employees to the appropriate tasks. Now that you're building and nurturing them, they will align themselves more loyally with the future of the company.

In addition to your advisors and mentors, the Power Tools you'll utilize will include the organizational chart that you've already developed and the policy and procedure manuals we've already mentioned. You'll need to revisit your MV²P Planning™ and benchmarking with your strategic partners. What progress have you made thus far? To make it to Stage 4, you'll need to assess where you are not making progress and address those areas aggressively.

CROSS-TRAINING FOR THE FUTURE

Another Power Tool you'll need is cross training. For long-term efficiency, you'll want to train key individuals in more than one area, in case of an emergency. Just like the military, you want to create redundancy in the organization. This is easier to accomplish in Stage 3 than it is after you've experienced huge growth in your market share.

Cross training helps with two challenges. First, it teaches employees to value everyone else's contribution. It is natural to think your job is the hardest and everyone else's is easy, especially if they are doing it well. Once your employees get a taste of someone else's world for a day, they'll learn to appreciate one another pretty quickly.

As you begin to implement your systems, you will discover that there are two basic types of employees. I like to call these muddy-water fish and clean-water fish. Just as in nature there are muddy-water fish that thrive when others can't see through the muck, there are employees in whom crisis brings out the best. While others are foundering in

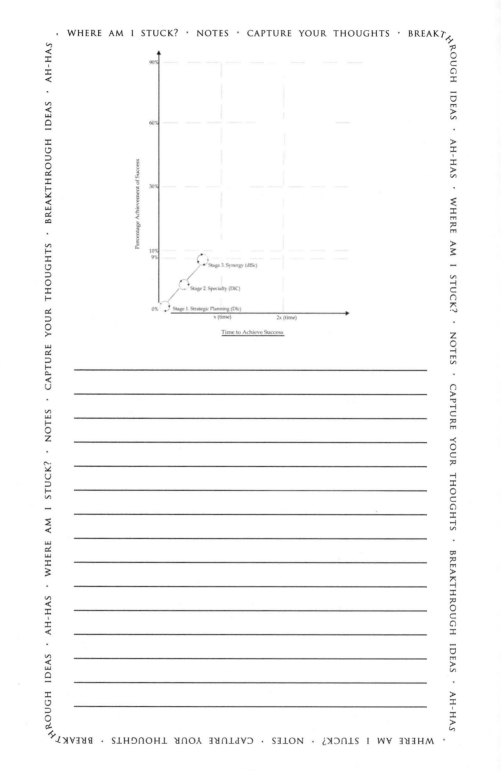

confusion, these employees rise above the fray and execute with ease. Because Stages 1, 2 and 3 are very chaotic, they shine during this time.

You're about to enter Stage 4. The water is about to become a lot clearer. Now your clean-water fish will rise to the top and the flaws of your muddy- water fish will be exposed. As soon you clearly articulate the policies and procedures, some muddy- water fish begin to squirm. They thrive in crisis because of the freedom it affords them. When roles are clearly defined, you may find that many excuse themselves from your organization.

You may be a muddy-water fish yourself. You thrived in the first stages and the people who have helped you get to this point did, too. In order to thrive and become a Stage 4, 5, 6 and 7 business, you have to clean up the water. And, unfortunately, most of the muddy-water fish will have to go. You will rarely need to fire them; they will leave on their own. Once exposed, they will feel insecure, which they hate (and so do you!). Be careful not to get rid of all of them, however. They still have a use. You need to discover, develop and deploy the right muddy-water fish to handle the muddy-water activities, namely sales and marketing.

This is why your employees must be cross trained in many areas. Prepare for a mass exodus of your muddy-water fish and stay patient. The sailing is about to get a lot smoother.

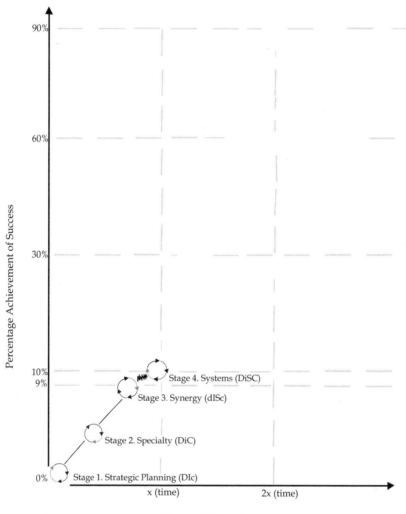

Percentage Achievement of Success

90%

60%

30%

10%
9%

0%

Stage 4. Systems (DiSC)

Stage 3. Synergy (dISc)

Stage 2. Specialty (DiC)

Stage 1. Strategic Planning (DIc)

x (time)   2x (time)

Time to Achieve Success

THE SYSTEMS STAGE

"A True Business Is Born"

You've made it! You're 18 months into the journey. You've written out your vision. You've completed your MV²P Planning™; You've become a specialist. You're an expert and an authority in your field. You survived the Synergy Stage and mastered the rules of the sandbox: You know how to play nice with others. For a while there, you were working harder than you ever thought you'd work in your life for what seemed to be less reward than you got at your old job.

Now, the tables have turned. You made it through the Miracle 1% and reached the point only a small portion of businesses will ever see. Welcome to Stage 4, the Systems Stage. Utilize your Power Tools at Stage 4 and you will be disproportionately and positively rewarded for the effort you put forth in Stages 1, 2 and 3. You will make a lot more money than the effort you put in. You will have more flexibility in your schedule for personal pursuits such as travel, time for yourself. You will move quickly and efficiently from Stage 4 to Stage 7.

This is where a true business is born. Up to this point, you really have had a job. Now you have a true business. How do you know? You're ready for systems. You're ready to take the policies and procedures manual you wrote in Stage 3 and put it to use.

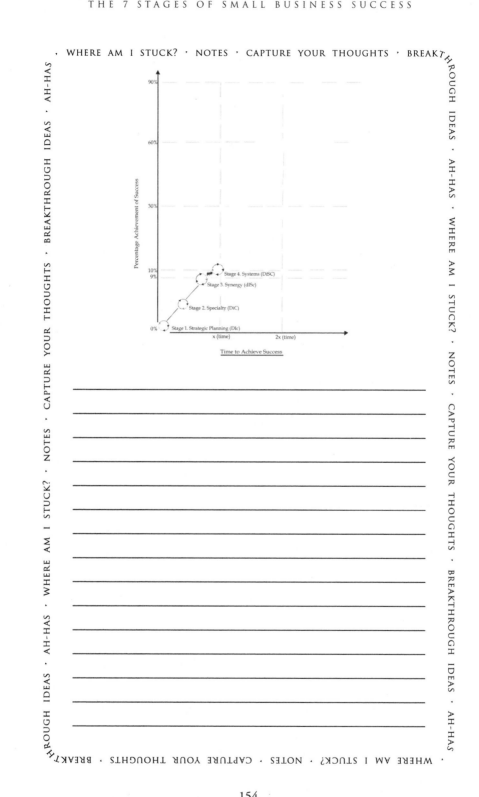

It's not unlike teaching your daughter how to ride a bicycle. You put on the training wheels for a while. You run right behind her all the way with your hand on the seat just to make sure she doesn't fall and hurt herself. Soon you move the wheels up a notch or two, so they're rarely touching the ground anymore. You ease up on your grip, and even run beside her without holding on. You are allowing her to learn how to ride on her own. That's how you're going to implement your systems. You're going monitor everything pretty closely for a while, but all the time you're preparing your departments to run those systems on their own.

The Systems Stage is one of the most personally rewarding of all the 7 Stages. Your employees will grow into their jobs. There will be a few bumps and bruises along the way, but soon you'll see them soar. Your investment in the automation of the business and the employees who implement the systems will pay huge dividends in increased revenue, time savings, and your ability to return to doing what you love to do in the business.

WHAT IS A SYSTEM?

My practical definition of a system is any activity or group of activities that can run on its own. That means that you can remove yourself from it and it will still run on its own. Remember way back when, we were talking about the DISCoverY process and we said, "Every job has a personality. Every industry has a personality." In your business, each position will begin to assume its own personality.

Systems by their very nature are predictable, consistent and reliable. They're scheduled and very structured. Initially, they will seem to slow

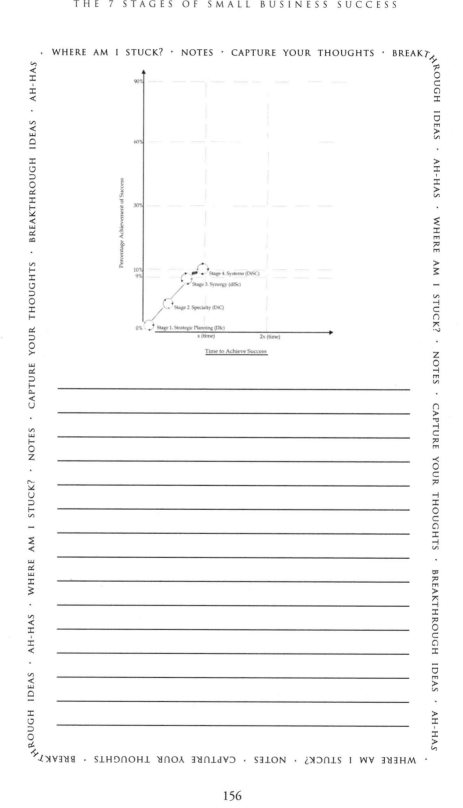

the pace of the business. It takes time for everyone to adjust to a set way of doing things, when up to this point they had been simply responding to you. Just as you were being patient with yourself in Stage 3, it's now time to be patient with others, including your staff. For your systems to take root, you need to stay the course.

STAGE 4 OUTCOMES, UPS AND DOWNS

Stage 4 is where you begin to reap significant rewards from your early efforts. In the early part of this stage, you may notice your sales. That's your blind spot for this stage, and it's a functional problem. To save yourself time in the long run, you are focusing extra attention on your employees. Meanwhile, the employees are turning extra attention to learning the systems. Just like teaching your daughter to ride her bike, you stay right beside them to ensure that they build enough confidence to do it on their own.

As you begin to manage these systems, your sales will start to increase exponentially. Your outcome for this stage is to implement these systems and allow them work on their own to the point where they develop their own personalities.

The bookkeeper's job has to develop its own personality, which means consistency and predictability. It's time for you to stop coming into the office early one day a week to write the checks as fast as you can, and then coming home late that night to staple the receipts. This is the stage where you will get out to your son's ball game or date night with your spouse. No more running into the office on a Saturday morning to get some bookkeeping work done before the family barbecue. It's time to let those systems soar.

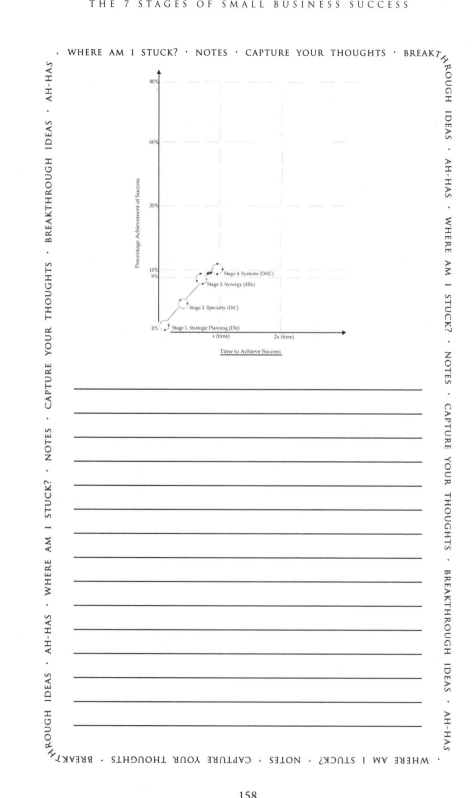

Remember that the muddy water is clearing up. Every day in Stage 4, you are slowing the pace. You come in and look at your tasks for the day. You execute those tasks in such a way that you can set your watch by what the people in your office are doing. You should be able to determine the day of the week by which task you tackle. Marketing? It must be Monday. Paychecks being printed? It must be Friday.

Systems are the foundation for long-term profitability and sustainability. Systems allow the employees to cut the umbilical cord from the owner. Systems allow your employees to reach their full potential. A system well-defined is a task half-solved. A well-defined system empowers and enables your employees to take initiative, solve problems on their own, and increase the short-term effectiveness and long-term efficiency of their job.

POWER TOOLS FOR STAGE 4

Your power tools for Stage 4 will lead you to Stage 5: Increasing your I^3Q or Intelligent, Incremental Improvements to Quality. You improve your quality by tweaking your automated functions, computerizing tasks, and refining your processes. These are incremental improvements: Each one builds on the last. Think smart, be intelligent.

This will help you obtain better results with little or no additional resources. A novice runner would probably collapse trying to run a marathon. Yet someone who incrementally increases his running distance can improve a great deal with very small increases in effort.

Small adjustments mean big impact over time. For example, have office supplies delivered rather than running off to the store whenever you run short on paper clips; have your server automatically filter your mails into

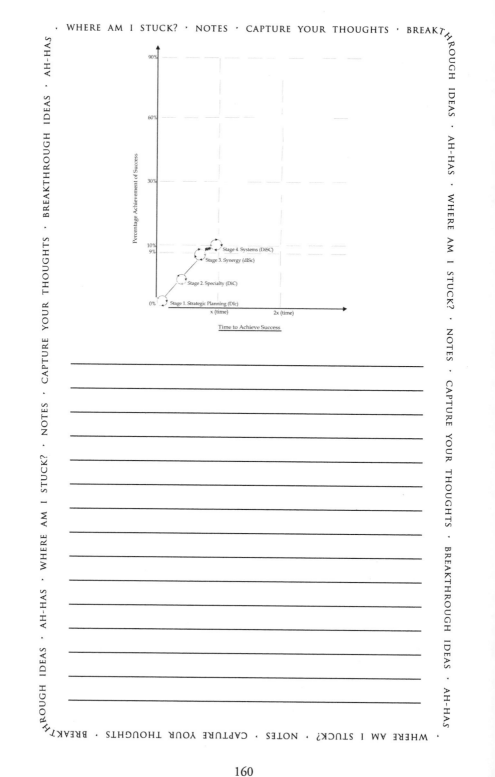

predetermined categories to save you the time of sorting low-priority correspondence; purchase equipment that reduces the need for unnecessary human intervention; outsource functions (payroll, marketing, etc.) to specialists who can do the work faster and cheaper than you can. Reduce your fixed costs and transfer them over to variable costs. Cut any unnecessary cost, no matter how small or insignificant it may seem. You must anticipate the needs of your organization and fulfill those needs in advance.

Whatever the area, you can make it better. That means processes, people, products, planning. This includes revisiting your MV²P Planning™, just as you did in Stage 3. Use the wealth of experience and insight you've garnered to refine those plans.

Part of your focus is measuring and monitoring all of your systems. Thus your Power Tools are incremental improvements in all areas. Just seek to make each area of your business 1% better. These are what I call Intelligent Incremental Improvements to Quality (I³Q). You don't have to make radical changes. Simply ask yourself what would make certain processes work a little better. In the middle of Stage 4, you should expect to see your systems improving, but you won't know this is happening unless you're monitoring them consistently.

Judge your systems by the results they achieve. Don't get distracted by the level of comfort or discomfort you feel while implementing those systems. You've heard the expression "no pain, no again." Systematizing your business qualifies as "some pain, all gain." For example, writing down job descriptions and a delegation plan might seem tedious. But having clear roles and responsibilities and a systematic approach to the delegation of those roles and responsibilities will allow your employees and subcontractors to take initiative, solve problems on their own,

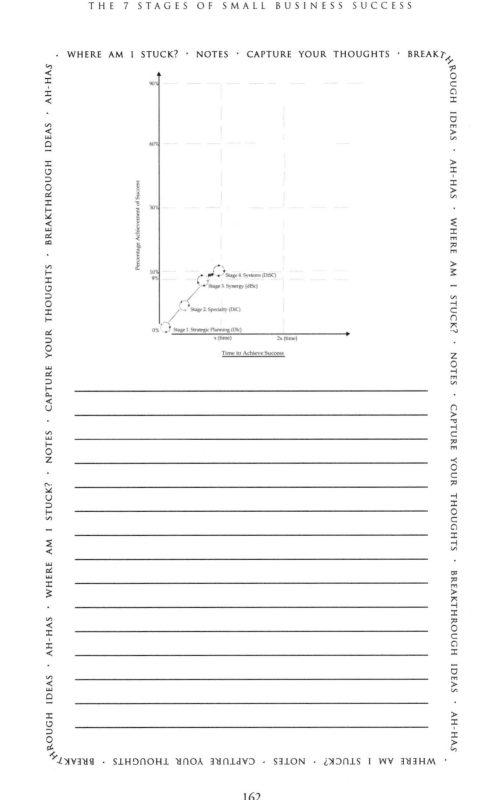

rather than constantly running to you. Having regular meetings to discuss your written critical success factors may not be sexy, but the results sure are.

One of my clients – I'll call him Jared – was a 74- year-old structural engineer who had been in business for 49 years. His goal was to transition the business to his grandson within the next five years. To ensure that the staff was taken care of properly and that the business would flourish post-transition, I suggested that we assemble Jared's key advisors to discuss our strategy going forward. Jared was very reluctant to do so; and I was about to find out why. He and I painstakingly created an agenda for the meeting, and prepared the questions and the topics that were to be discussed.

On the day of the meeting, my colleague David opened by introducing everyone. He laid out the agenda and the objective for the meeting, which was to transition the business to Jared's grandson while maintaining stability for the staff. I could sense the tension building in Jared. David handed the floor to Jared's longtime attorney, who recited all of the reasons that this wouldn't work as desired and listed a myriad of seemingly insurmountable legal and corporate hurdles. Next up was Jared's longtime accountant, who went through the gamut of tax implications. Before the accountant even finished, Jared whispered to me, "This is why I was so reluctant to have this meeting." I asked, "Is this how your accountant and attorney usually communicate with each other?" Jared replied, "They have never been in the same room together before."

Something needed to change in this meeting, and fast. I asked the advisors at the table, "May we adopt the idea that this transition will go through, and that we reframe our objective to determining how we

163

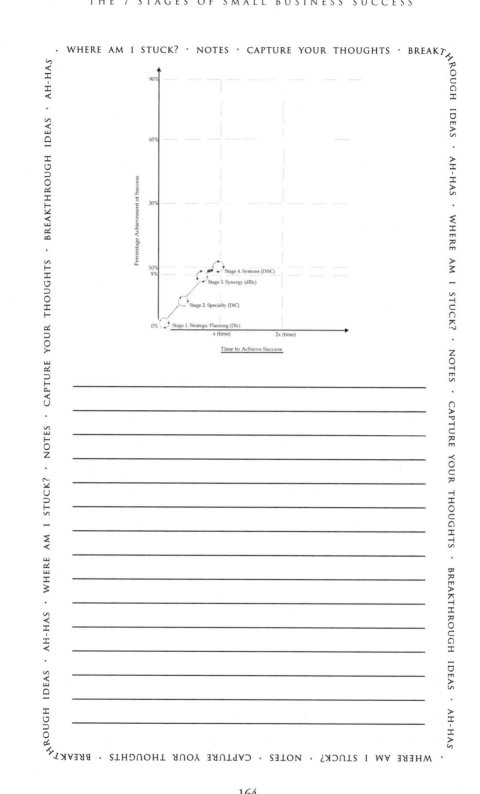

will we make this transition happen in a way that minimizes downside risk and maximizes the upside potential for the future?" With that agreement and our redirected focus, we methodically went around the table and brainstormed ideas to make this plan a reality. Before systems, it was a free-for-all with no result. With our systematic preparation and methodical approach in this and subsequent meetings, Jared achieved his objective. Painful? Uncomfortable? Maybe so. The outcome was worth the discomfort, and the firm has enjoyed years of growth as a result.

In your business, maybe the customer service procedures weren't popular with the staff at first. Do they work? Are they making the customers happy? Then stick with them. I recently went to a café and ordered one of their beverages for take-out. As I drove down the road and took my first sip (I needed to let it cool down a bit), I realized I was given the wrong drink. On my return trip I passed the café again and stopped in. I explained to the server what happened. Without hesitation or explanation, the server asked me what drink I originally ordered. She quickly took my order and replaced the drink. As she handed me my drink, she apologized for the inconvenience and handed me a voucher for a free drink for the next time I returned. I noticed in particular the relief, and joy, on her face when she confidently handed me the voucher knowing that this policy would make me a happy camper. Everybody wins and I do intend to go back!

In our office for example, we created how-to manuals for each of our training programs. They document virtually every part of the process. This then enabled us to create a standardized template on which all of our training programs can run. We have eliminated the last-minute dramas that had once been part of preparing for a training seminar. The preparation of the program had been so stressful that the actual

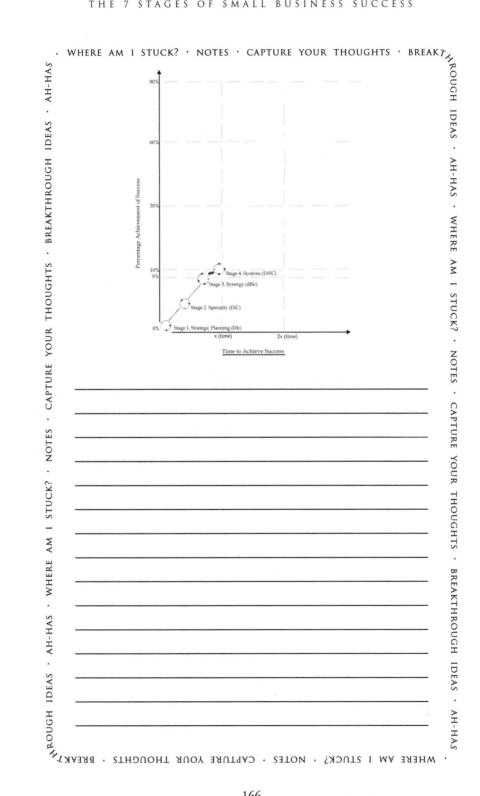

event was anticlimactic. We were all exhausted! By contrast, we can now enjoy the event and provide a more memorable experience for those in attendance.

This will be an uncomfortable stage. Systems are probably what you avoided in your last job or endeavor, which is all the more reason to embrace them right now. Look at the results of your systems dispassionately. If you're getting the result you want, do more of it. If you're not, change it.

Once you get toward the end of Stage 4, you want to turn your attention again to improving quality. You're now at the stage where your daughter doesn't need you right beside her all the time. You're in the same room with your employees, of course, keeping an eye on them. However, you no longer have to review everything or look over their shoulders constantly. The training wheels are off and they're riding on their own.

I^3Q is the methodology that will become our culture in Stage 5.

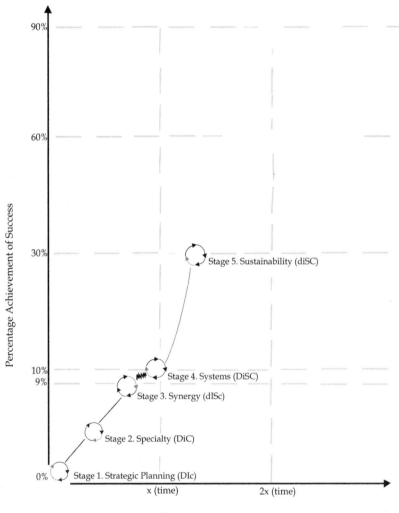

Percentage Achievement of Success

Time to Achieve Success

THE
SUSTAINABILITY STAGE

"A Franchise Is Born"

Y ou have now created the type of business that is proven. You have replicated yourself and your systems, which are running on their own. The superiority of your systems has caused your clients come back to you over and over again. You can even start thinking about expansion.

You know you are a Stage 5 business when you begin to be complimented for *things other than your product or service*. For example, Starbucks is known not just for coffee, but also for the experience: the music it plays in its stores, the water it sells, and the children it sends aid to. McDonald's is known for its speed, consistency and the merchandise (toys) that accompanies its meals. The systems that each of these companies have created and implemented have been perfected let the customers appreciate things other than the companies' core offerings.

Remember that your product or service is a commodity. Someone else can replicate your product and have it on the market in six months, as Timothy Ferriss noted in "The 4-Hour Workweek." It is the relationship you create with your customers that is priceless and timeless. The Unique Customer Experience™ that you create cannot be stolen, replicated or matched. In the book "The Southwest Airlines Way," author Jody Hoffer Gittell chronicled Southwest's ability to create

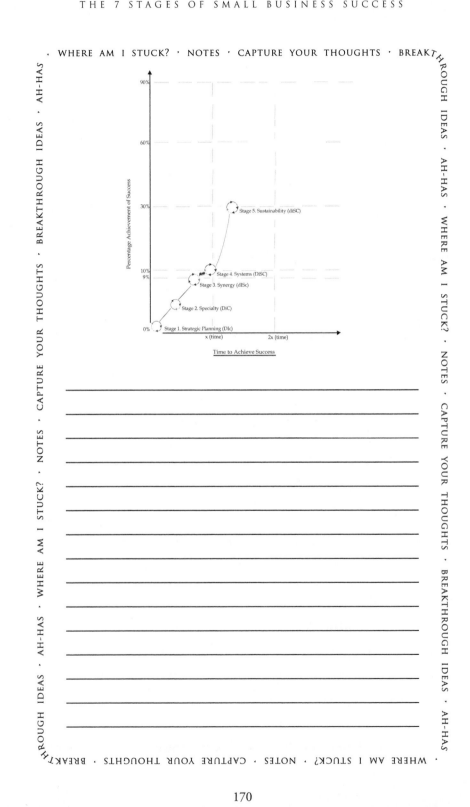

Stage 5. Sustainability (diSC)

Stage 4. Systems (DISC)

Stage 3. Synergy (dISc)

Stage 2. Specialty (DiC)

Stage 1. Strategic Planning (DIc)

Percentage Achievement of Success

90%

60%

30%

10%
9%

0%

x (time)   2x (time)

Time to Achieve Success

a unique rapport with its employees as well as its customers. Other airlines attempted to duplicate Southwest's success and failed because they could not match Southwest's culture. The vision of Southwest Airline is so bold and well-defined (to be the lowest-cost airline in each market) that it has trickled down through the entire organization.

I once took a trip via Southwest with my wife and then-18-month-old daughter. We arrived at the terminal with our six suitcases, car seat, baby stroller, toys and carry-on bag filled with diapers, formula and baby food. I was happy to see that Southwest offered curbside baggage check-in. Normally, the curbside check-in operators wait for the passengers to approach the kiosk. Not this time. The Southwest representative, a petite woman, came up and offered to help us with our bags. I felt bad, as the bags were bigger and heavier than she was. She insisted and said, "Don't worry sir, you have your hands full and a flight to catch. Just follow me and we'll have you on your way in no time." Then she said something that stood out: "Besides Mr. Gould, *we only make money when our planes are in the air.*"

We made our way to our departure gate, where I noticed a long line of people waiting to board. A flight attendant came from behind the boarding counter and began to guide us to the boarding queue. "Will we need to stand in that long line?" "No, Mr. Gould, I am walking you over to our preboarding area. Please wait here with your family and we will call you *first* to give you an opportunity to choose your seat and get settled in properly. We want you to have the time you need to get comfortable while making sure we can board everyone else to ensure an on-time departure." And then he said, *"We only make money when the plane is in the air."*

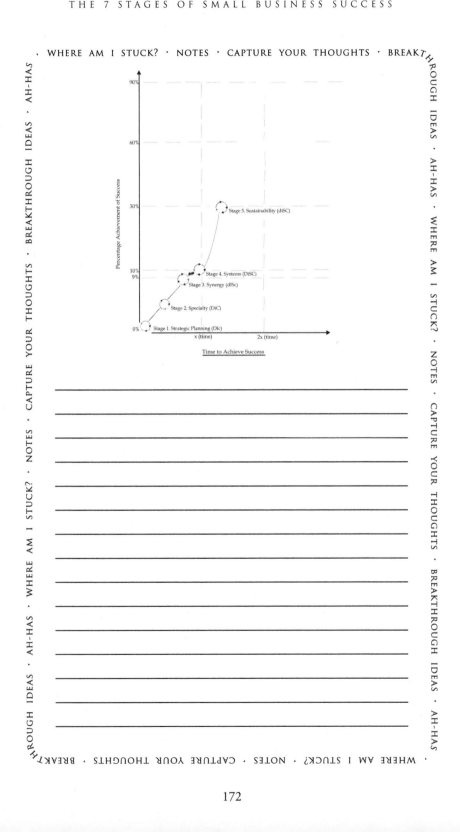

I could sense that hearing that expression again was more than a coincidence. I never moved so quickly through an airport, and yet never felt rushed. Systems, systems, systems. The result of a relentless pursuit to perfect your systems is a unique client experience, one that positively affected me enough to write about it here.

As you perfect your systems, you are potentially building lifetime loyalty in your customers. Whether you legally formed a franchise entity or not, your company has mastered the systematic approach to delivering a consistent and enjoyable experience to its customers over and over again. As mentioned earlier, and according to the book *The Starbucks Experience*, the average Starbucks customer visits the store 18 out of 20 working days per month. The significant consistent product and experience that people have when they go to a Starbucks have built an incredible rate of loyalty among the customer base. That is what a franchise is all about.

Your Stage 5 business is sustainable because your systems are running the show. They are the rock stars of Stage 5 and they can now outlast you. The business will reflect your vision, yet it expresses that vision in its own distinct way.

Now that your systems are *running* the business, you can get to work *leading* the business. Sales begin to grow exponentially because you're getting a lot of reward from a lot of different areas. Your repeatable processes mean a more significant and consistent experience and a deeper connection with your customers. People come to you now with expectations that this connection has established.

Your outcome in Stage 5 is strategic expansion. You're constantly asking yourself how you're going to build your business. How are you going to make your operation expand and grow? Part of your expansion plan

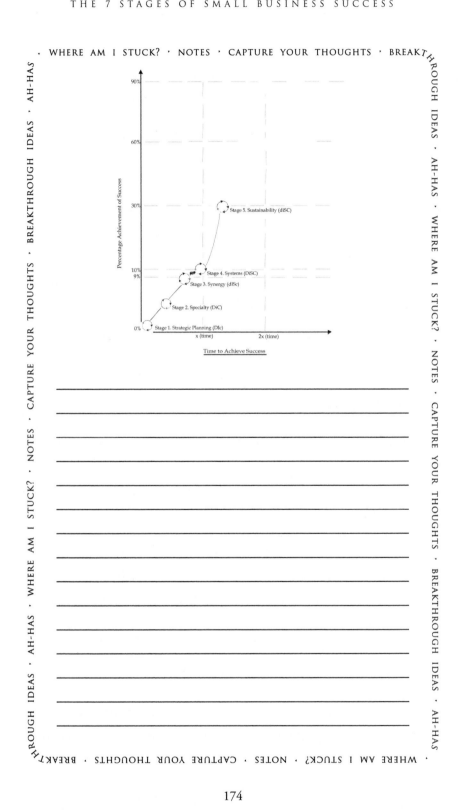

might even be pondering your exit. We'll talk more about your exit strategy later.

Your focus in this stage is creating a culture of I³Q (Intelligent, Incremental Improvements to Quality). How do you do that? You're going to evaluate virtually every process in your business on a regular basis. You're going to provide feedback and continual coaching to your employees. You'll tell them what they did well and what they can do to take their performance and results to the next level. Then you'll offer them support and resources to make that happen.

In Stage 5, small improvements make a big difference. Changing a key phrase in an advertisement can generate extra leads; asking one question to a customer shows a genuine and sincere interest in him or her as a person; automating one point in your processes can lead to fewer defects and quality shortfalls in the long term.

The reality is that most franchise locations will not reach their full potential. A franchise gives you the framework for success, but it is you who needs to follow through consistently. You cannot ignore Stages 1-4 just because you are at Stage 5. A passionate owner with an aligned staff who methodically and joyfully executes their daily tasks drives the Sustainability Stage. That culture creates the environment for the end user, the customer, to enjoy a superb experience each and every time. The end user is not the franchisor's customer, but your customer. It is your job as the franchise location owner to create that unique customer experience. There will always be local nuances, and you will have to consider the dynamics that are distinct to the community you serve.

This is why systems are so important. When the basic functions of the business are standardized and well-ingrained in your employees'

· WHERE AM I STUCK? · NOTES · CAPTURE YOUR THOUGHTS · BREAKTHROUGH IDEAS · AH-HAS

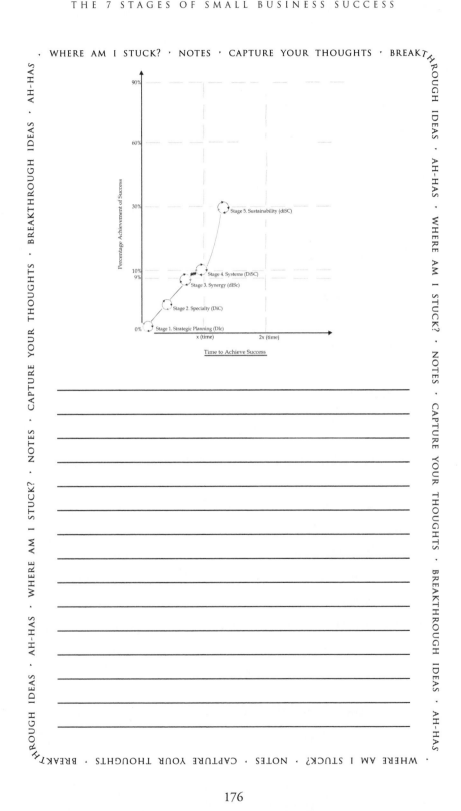

minds, the workers can then focus on the customer, making sure they receive the service and support they deserve.

Why do some franchises fail? I have advised a number of franchisors, from North America to South Africa to Australia to Europe, and the lament is the same: The franchisees deviate from the system. I have seen franchisees treat their enterprise like a job and not like a business. They don't follow through consistently with the changes at each stage. They refuse to stop micromanaging their employees, even after those employees help design the systems and become fully trained in their operation. You, as the owner, do not need to be driving everything anymore. You can let go, and you must.

One of my clients, a high-tech franchisor in Australia, has more than 25 locations throughout that country. I attended a recent meeting of the franchisees in Sydney. The franchisor opened the meeting by sharing examples of the franchisees that were following the systematic approach AND provided outstanding customer service. Those franchisees were by far the more successful locations. The least successful franchisees? Those who deviated from the systematic approach AND were not focusing on the unique customer experience.

As you set your employees free from your prison of micromanagement, you will be able to utilize the systems to create incremental improvements in all areas. You can no longer effectively dictate every part of the business, so the only way to improve quality is to allow the systems to drive the business.

Now that the machinery is *running*, how do you *lead* the business? Your two jobs are to manage your cash flow and seek growth opportunities for your business. Your Power Tool for Stage 5 is benchmarking. It's time to revisit all those financial targets and see where you are. How

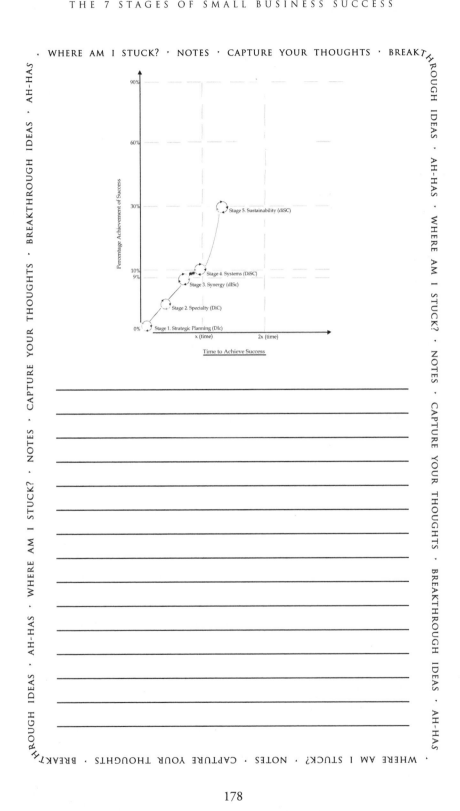

are you stacking up to the industry standard? Are you becoming tops in your field yet? Before you expand, you want to make sure that you're following your industry very closely so you know what will be expected of your company. It is essential to know who is tops in your field and how they manage their numbers. It is at this juncture where you revisit financial benchmarking. Learn how you compare against the competition. Advances at this stage are incremental. Little improvements mean big gains because they can be broadcast across multiple business functions and/or locations. Walmart made the simple decision to place a door greeter to engage customers as they entered the store. One tiny decision, broadcast across all of their locations, adds up to an increased customer experience company wide.

Internally, it's the time for performance-based incentives. These can include nonmonetary bonuses and recognition such as Employee of the Month awards. You also want to build your presence in the community by getting your employees involved in charitable causes, or hosting company events attached to some worthy cause.

As you stay abreast of industry expectations, start to look into licensing, franchising, affiliate programs, joint ventures, and other types of networking. This is also the time to design new products and upgrade services, building on all your success so far.

Stage 5 lays the foundation for the business to run itself. You know you're in Stage 5 when you can leave your business for two months or more and find it running well (if not better) upon your return. And when you return, you read testimonials from happy customers who are complimenting you for the experience they had that was over and above the functionality of your product or service. That's a very good feeling.

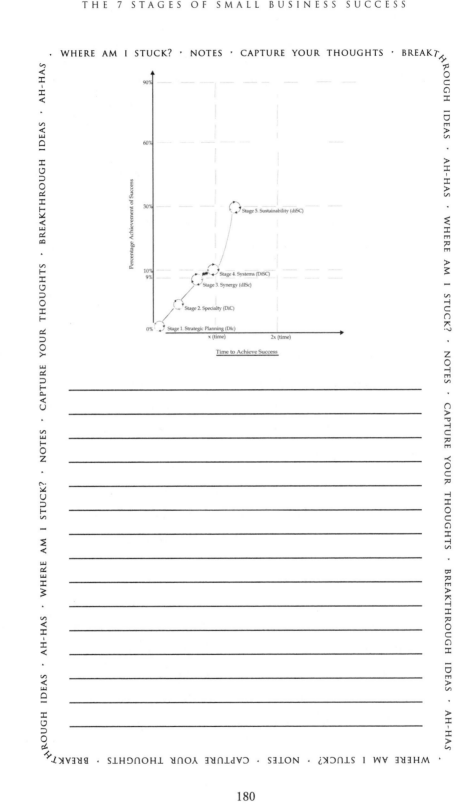

Stage 5 is of particular interest to entrepreneurial clients because it means you have constructed a solid foundation for expansion. Now is the time to open that new location, license your product, franchise your idea, or create an affiliate program, joint venture or a partnership, etc. You have properly managed your growth to the point that you are truly ready for expansion. To grow prematurely and too fast could mean that run the risk of running out of cash. Business is a cash game. If you are out of cash, you are out of the game. Once you are ready for expansion, the financial rewards are huge. Richard Branson has licensed the Virgin brand name to more than 200 products, services and companies, according to Alan Deutschman's *Business the Branson Way*, making him a billionaire. The franchise/licensing business model has proven to be one the most successful business models. One in 12 businesses in the United States is a franchise business, Karl Gibbons says in *Franchising, the Way Forward?* They work because systems work. The blind spot for franchise locations is mediocrity, because systems are made so the average worker can perform in them. Business success comes from developing efficient systems, retaining effective people, and providing a Unique Customer Experience™ that keeps them coming back for more.

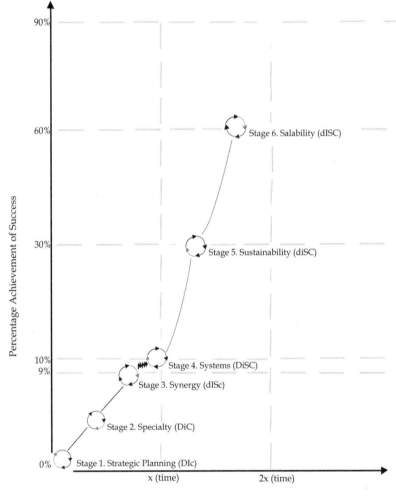

90%

60% · · · · · · · · · · · Stage 6. Salability (dISC)

Percentage Achievement of Success

30% · · · · · · Stage 5. Sustainability (diSC)

Stage 4. Systems (DiSC)
10%
9%
Stage 3. Synergy (dISc)

Stage 2. Specialty (DiC)

0% Stage 1. Strategic Planning (DIc)

x (time)   2x (time)

Time to Achieve Success

THE SALABILITY STAGE

"An Asset Is Born!"

Hang in there, we're almost done. We've instilled a culture of I³Q. We've created the systems and they're sustainable. We've expanded our business to multiple locations, franchised it, or rolled out sequel products or affiliate programs. Welcome to Stage 6.

Your blind spot in Stage 6 is complacency: We can't put the business on cruise control just yet. This is tempting. After all, we've put everything in place; why can't we can just kick back and enjoy it? There's still a little more work to do.

During Stage 6, you've got three of your four quadrants running very high: You'll notice on the graph that D is still very low, just like it was in Stage 5. The systems and controls are still driving the business. Sales have increased exponentially. While others who reach this point would party and call it a day, we're going to make sure we take this business all the way to Stage 7 success.

There are two things you must keep in mind in Stage 6. First, sales should be steady and increasing. If you let sales dip at this point, it is a dysfunctional problem at best and a crisis at worst. Second, be sure you stay married to your MV²P Planning™. Although you're expanding now, you still need to "dance with the one who brung you" as the old saying goes. Your mission, vision, values and purpose brought you this

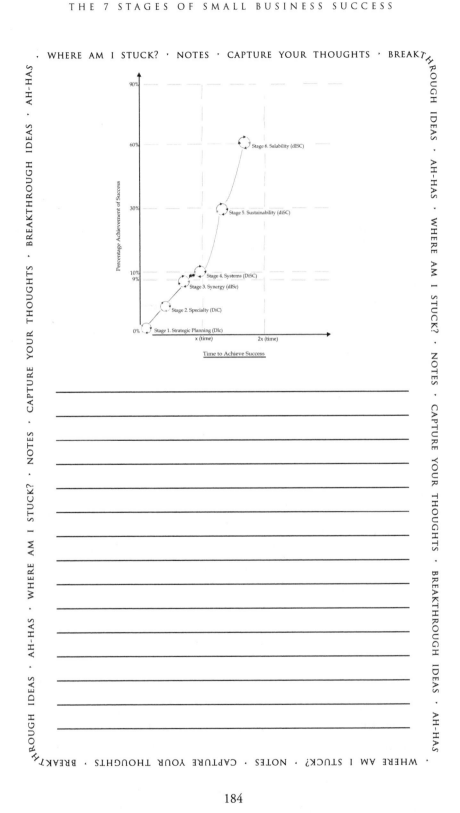

far. Don't lose sight of them now. By this point, your mission statement should be accepted and believed in by everyone in the company. When they all know it by heart, you'll know that your programs and enhancements have successfully permeated the entire organization.

What is your outcome in Stage 6? Simply put: cosmetic enhancements. You're still staying focused on your planning and you have your eye on your sales targets and milestones planning. Now you want to upgrade your products, their look and the company's image. It might be time to update the building or to order new uniforms. We may upgrade the logo, as a lot of companies do. These are little image enhancements with a larger goal in mind.

The purpose of these improvements is to keep the company on the cutting edge of the marketplace and to reassert its place as an industry leader. All this will raise the tangible and intangible value of the business you've worked so hard to create.

SALES AND SALABILITY

During Stage 6, your focus has returned to sales. We want them moving upward as much as or more than ever before. We want those books looking very shiny and those financial statements to be the envy of everyone out there. It's time to make sure that the business is not only profitable, but also credit- worthy and investor-friendly, making it attractive to financial institutions, private investors, or anyone with cash. This is the stage where our business becomes salable: Our star has been born.

Stage 6 is *not* the time to overhaul the organization, redo the leadership structure, or make radical changes to those systems. These are *cosmetic*

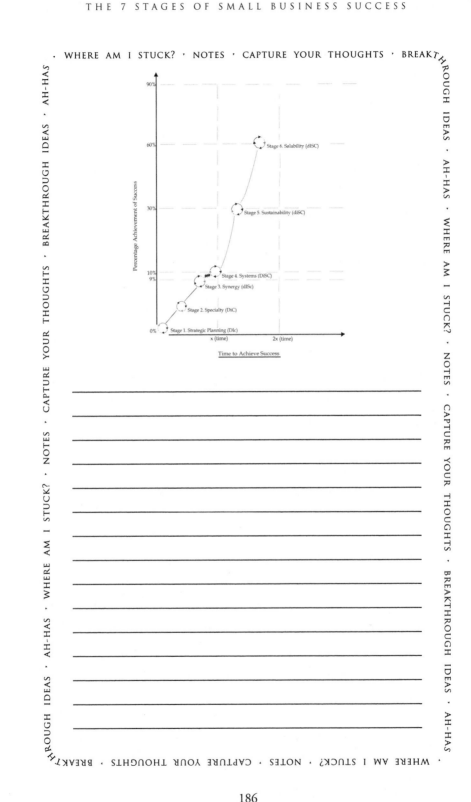

enhancements: We're talking a little blush and lip gloss, not a crash diet and liposuction.

When preparing your business for salability, you want to make sure you leave highly trained talent behind. It is not just cash flow that interests potential investors and lenders, but also the leadership team that has been groomed to manage that cash flow. Whether or not you really intend to sell, part of what makes your business valuable is the fact that it no longer relies on your efforts and energy. In the latter part of Stage 6, you want to focus on your executives, leadership team and key employees. You want to confirm they are not only in alignment but that they are also continuing to build their core competencies. This ensures your quality will continue to increase even after you're gone.

This is also the stage to revisit your milestone planning. Have you achieved what you thought you would achieve at this point? Were you able to reach each milestone in the intended time frame? You're in the home stretch, so it's important to ask yourself the tough questions. By Stage 6, cash flow and profit should be high. The systems and controls are still driving the business, so there may be times when you feel you get away from your vision. While this is a functional problem of the stage, you want to get back on track as quickly as possible.

KNOW YOUR WORTH

Stage 6 is almost like a second honeymoon with the business. Minor adjustments yield sales increases, while strong systems and controls allow you to have your own life. When you put your advisory board together in Stage 1, we talked about having somebody who is an expert in business valuations. This individual can now tell you what your

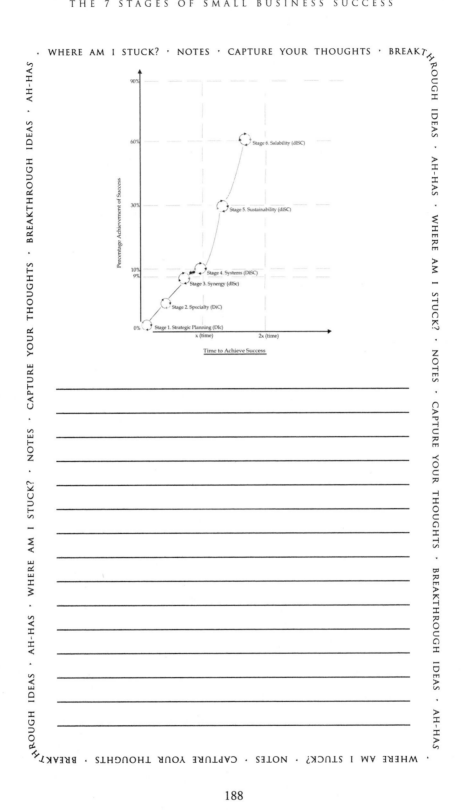

business is worth. One of your Stage 6 Power Tools is a full valuation of the business. This is an add-on and a logical extension of the benchmarking that you've already done. Are you getting the value for all that hard work? What can you tweak to make the business more saleable?

There are many strategies you can employ when selling your business. Maybe you're on the verge of taking your business public. In this case, you want to surround yourself with experts who can bring you to an initial public offering (IPO). You might also decide to merge with or acquire another company.

The tangible analysis of your business is fairly straightforward: It is simply the assessments, benchmarking, attributes that we talked about earlier. Do an exhaustive asset analysis of your business, leaving no stone unturned, to make sure that you are aware of the value of everything in your inventory. I can guarantee you that outsiders are starting to evaluate the worth of your company by this stage, so make sure you are ahead of the game.

You will soon learn that even if you have no intention of selling your business, people will offer to buy it. If you're profitable and well-run, this is inevitable. Back in my construction company days, when we were building custom homes, invariably, during the course of construction, people would drive up and offer to buy the house. These houses were not for sale; we were building on contract for someone who had already purchased the home. Yet time and again individuals would approach us with their business card with a price on the back.

When I would tell the prospective buyer that I was not the owner, he would inevitably ask me to pass the offer on to the owner to see if he would sell. Many times, that offer was higher than what the home was worth. Obviously, it was important for the owner to know what

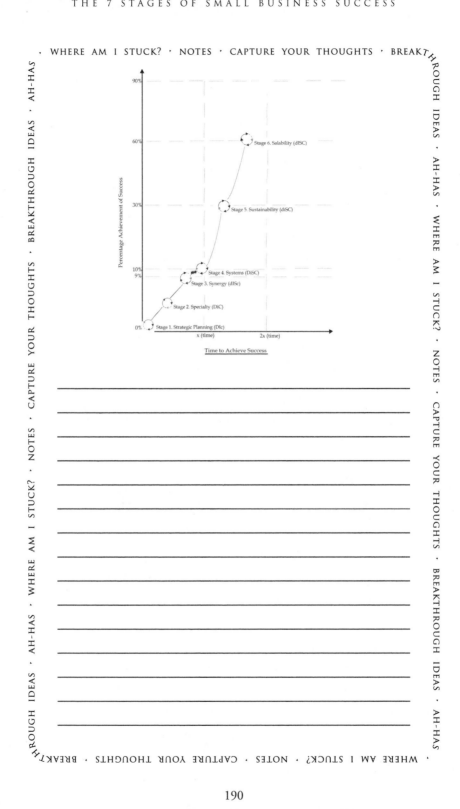

the home was worth to know whether to even entertain any of these offers. You want to be aware of what your business is worth by Stage 6, because offers will come, whether you solicit them or not.

Remember, only a small percentage of businesses ever reach this stage, and when they do, people are watching. Some of them will be willing to overpay for your success. If your business is well-run and you have been following the stages, your business will sell for a premium. If you have not been following my advice, you can still sell your business. However, you might sell at a discount, meaning you will have very little to show for all your hard work.

So, you could be disproportionately and positively rewarded for your efforts. Back in Stages 1, 2 and 3, you were working hard and being paid less. You thought it would never end. Well, now you reap your reward. In Stage 6, the business that once took all your time is now a full-grown asset.

You are about to enter Stage 7. This is uncharted territory for 99% of the businesses out there. You've grown and developed a leadership team that will continually contribute to the value of the business beyond your efforts. You're about to fire yourself for the last time.

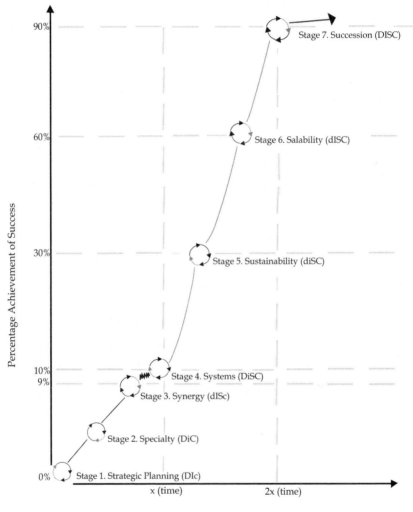

90% — Stage 7. Succession (DISC)

60% — Stage 6. Salability (dISC)

Percentage Achievement of Success

30% — Stage 5. Sustainability (diSC)

10% — Stage 4. Systems (DiSC)
9% — Stage 3. Synergy (dISc)

Stage 2. Specialty (DiC)

0% — Stage 1. Strategic Planning (DIc)

x (time)   2x (time)

Time to Achieve Success

THE SUCCESSION STAGE

"A Legacy Is Born!"

Congratulations. You are now in a position to have someone succeed you, which is the ultimate business success. As a matter of fact, many people start businesses with the express purpose of selling or donating it, while reaping the ongoing residual income it yields.

In Stage 7, your business is all things to all people. You'll notice on your graph that the capital D has finally returned: Direction is strong again. You still have robust sales and consistent systems. You still have quality products and controls. You are an MV²P™ business firing on all cylinders and in all your DISCoverY quadrants. Your employees (your internal customers) enjoy a culture of fulfillment and satisfaction with what they do. It aligns with their behaviors, priorities and personal strengths. Your vision has been realized.

Remember, you have been "firing" yourself upward every quarter for the last three years. You have one more job to lose and one more hire to make. Your potential Stage 7 blind spot is having no exit strategy. You must have an exit strategy, whether you actually plan to exit or not.

What's your next move for your business in Stage 7? Start by asking yourself about your next move in life. Remember when Bill Gates fired himself as CEO of Microsoft? He made himself the Chief Technology Officer. Then he fired himself again, so he could focus on his founda-

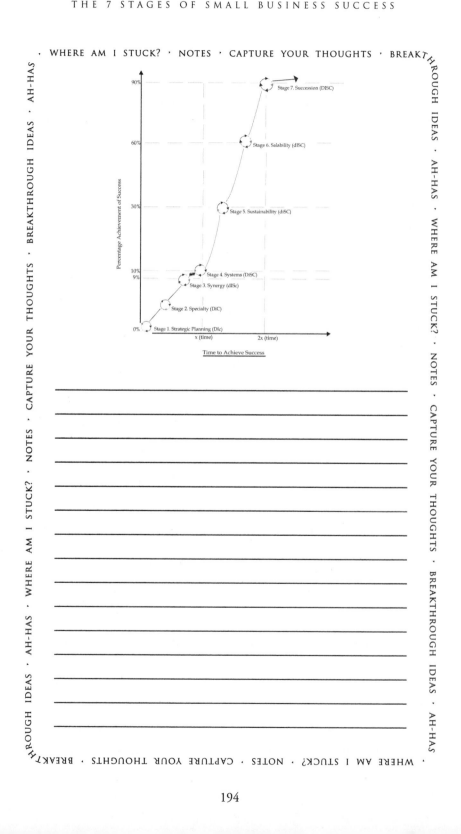

tion. You don't need to be Microsoft to be a Stage 7 company. You can be a micro-business and still reach the Succession Stage.

There is a little ice cream shop in my hometown that is a Stage 7 business. It is family-run, has four employees, and is celebrating its 50th anniversary. The owners have held the vision of being the best ice cream shop around, serving its customers faithfully and impeccably. They create an experience, too. When was the last time you enjoyed standing on line for something? When was the last time you **looked forward** to waiting on a line? Well, you will here; it's part of the experience. You'll see dads hoisting their children onto their shoulders; you'll see friends and colleagues who have stopped by for a treat; local sports teams will celebrate a victory (or soothe a defeat); families will travel down and "tailgate"; classic cars, motorcycles and vehicles of all types will come rolling in.

Notice that I haven't even mentioned the ice cream yet? I have been coming to this ice cream shop for more than 35 years, and my loyalty is NOT about the ice cream. I can get the same ice cream at the supermarket. I come again and again for the EXPERIENCE. The owners have done an excellent job of creating an enjoyable and consistent experience. As a result, people will line up outside in all types of weather to get their heard-earned ice cream. The beauty of the operation is that the success of the business lies in the product, the process and the experience, not with the owner. The business has created a legacy for itself that can be passed from generation to generation. It is a Stage 7 business.

What is your outcome for Stage 7? Believe it or not, your outcome is to create and answer the question: Now what? What is next for me in my life? What is next for me in my business? Your focus is to reconnect

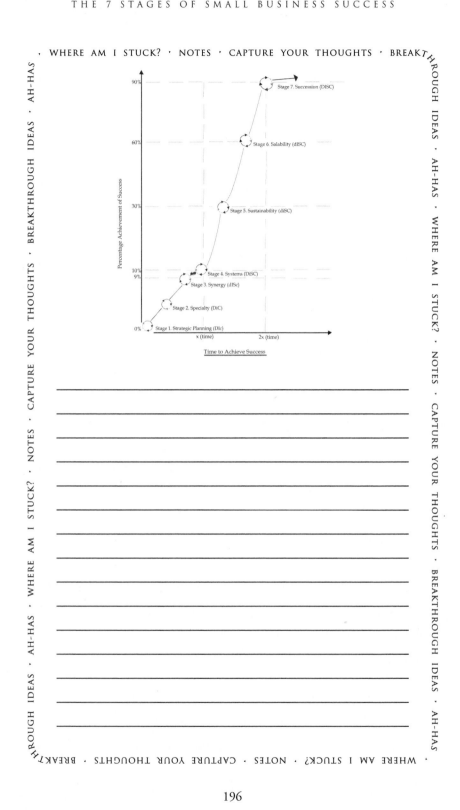

to that vision, direction and MV²P Planning™. Raise your banner and start to lead your industry. Others will follow you, because you are well-known and dominant in your market. Your widgets, people, processes and quality have developed optimally and are delivering consistent results.

There are many examples of some well-known Stage 7 businesses. Microsoft is an obvious Stage 7 business. The Beatles and Elvis Presley are Stage 7 businesses, because the tremendous success these artists achieved caused their names to live on beyond themselves.

More than album sales, they created a legacy by collaborating with other artists, and allowing others to record, remake and sample their songs. The other artists carry forth their legacies. When most musical acts stop touring and/or recording, their sales stall or decline. Not these two. They have become part of our lives and continue to impact us long after they are gone.

STAGE 7 IN ALL SIZES

When it comes to Stage 7, size doesn't matter. In my own hometown, I know a micro-business, a medium-size business and a larger business that are all Stage 7 companies. There is the tiny little ice cream shop that has been around for decades. People usually don't like to stand in lines anymore, but these customers are having such a significant experience that waiting in line is part of the fun. People know exactly what they're going to get at this shop and they keep coming back.

The sign at the ice cream shop says "family owned for the last fifty years," but I couldn't tell you who owns it. It's the same family that

· WHERE AM I STUCK? · NOTES · CAPTURE YOUR THOUGHTS · BREAKTHROUGH IDEAS · AH-HAS

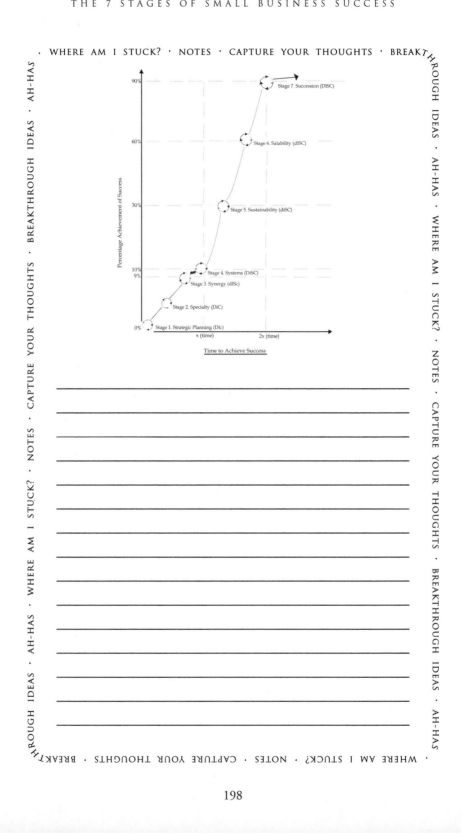

turned me down for a job when I was younger. The place has developed its own personality that has lived beyond its original owners.

It will never be a big business and it's not a franchise. You can only fit two or three people in the building at a time! Yet it's a Stage 7 business. It's already gone three generations. It will go a fourth and could be sold to anyone without a hitch. The new owner would be turning a profit immediately.

Now for my small business story: A garden center that has been around for about 80 years is well-known and employs about 20 people. In addition to doing good business, the owners actually grow crops on a percentage of their land, making it technically a farm. In the middle of the nondescript suburbs, this little farm delivers a significant experience to soccer moms and dads with outdoor grills. They love the feeling that they're getting a little bit of rural America in their own back yards. The farm has grown with the times by adding various products, but has stayed a small business by design.

It sits on eight acres of some of the most valuable land in the area. Every year, regardless of the economy, somebody will offer top dollar for that land because of its potential. The owners have been offered millions more than it's worth. Yet they are aware of the tangible and intangible worth the business has to them, so they've chosen not to sell. It's part of their family legacy. It's not part of their exit strategy to sell. It's part of each owner's strategy to pass it along to the next generation.

My favorite hometown shop is the kind of little hardware store that would normally be eliminated the moment a big box store comes into town. It actually sits on the road between the two national- chain home-improvement stores. When those two giants came to town, everyone worried it was over for this little shop. Surprisingly, the owners were

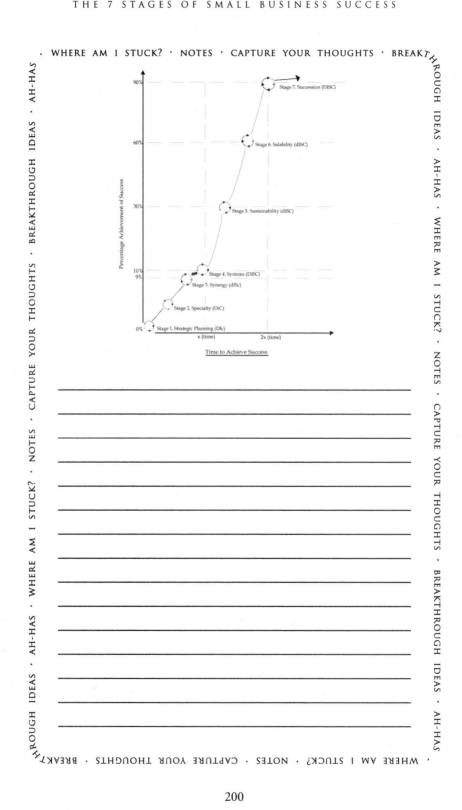

not worried because they had built their business on something no one else could match: outstanding service. This "small" business is actually the biggest business of its kind around. Employees know your name, why you were in there last, and want to know how you're enjoying that new deck you built last spring. No large chain can match that.

They retain the name of the family that began the store years ago, and enjoy the status of a local icon. Instead of suffering when the big-box stores moved in, their sales have remained robust, and they have continued to thrive. Other businesses in the area have dropped like flies, but this one is a Stage 7 business.

There are other organizations in which the owner has branded his name so well that it symbolizes a certain level of quality, such as the Trump Organization. Donald Trump has licensed his name to many projects all around the world. They use his name even though he is not the developer of the building, and that name has become the gold standard in the construction industry. This didn't just happen. Trump has created a Stage 7 business by purposefully and strategically positioning himself and creating his business identity. As a result, he is the highest-paid in his field, and he can sell and license his name and to create affiliations and joint ventures. Recently Trump redesigned his Web site to introduce the world to the "Next Generation;" Stage 7 in progress.

There are also very successful businesses that are not yet in Stage 7. Just as Microsoft is a Stage 7 business, Apple Computer is not. Why? It still relies on the creativity, image and vision of Steven Jobs. Whenever he has exited the business, its value has gone with him. In fact, the price of Apple stock has fluctuated based the health challenges that Jobs has faced since 2003. (The Star Ledger; "Apple Stock Goes Up as Jobs eases

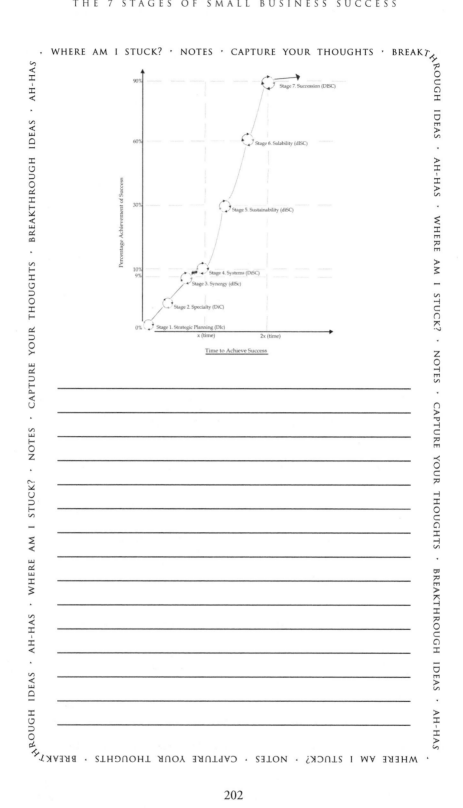

concerns" January 6, 2009.) Chrysler Motors has sought out strategic alliances for the last 30 years, without obtaining the results it intended. Chrysler continues to rely on the strategic alliance it has with others and has been unable, so far, to create a unique business identity.

Think about the Rolling Stones and Elton John. These are incredibly successful musicians, already in the Rock and Roll Hall of Fame. Yet, when they stop touring, their music, their popularity and their sales slow considerably. On the other hand, the Beatles are still among the highest grossing bands in the new millennium and they have not recorded an album together in more than 30 years. Elvis Presley still remains a very robust selling musician, 30 years after his death.

What do Elvis and the Beatles have that Elton and the Stones lack? Third-party validation that their music is timeless. If nobody ever copied a Beatles or Elvis tune, then their legacy would have faded along with everyone's memory of them. Movies, television programs and advertisements have used their music. Cover bands emulate their look and sounds. Broadway plays and other theatrical productions have been created and inspired by their legacy (Remember "Beatlemania" and the "Love" version of Cirque du Soleil? How about the movie "Honeymoon in Vegas" featuring the skydivers named the Flying Elvises – Utah Chapter? The Rolling Stones and Elton John have given me music; the Beatles and Elvis have become part of my consciousness because they have become part of my life. The Beatles and Elvis Presley are well-designed brands that have effectively worked their way into our daily culture. The Rolling Stones and Elton John, while wildly successful, remain musical acts.

A Stage 7 business actually increases in value as it relies less on the owner. This comes from strong leadership, strong products with a

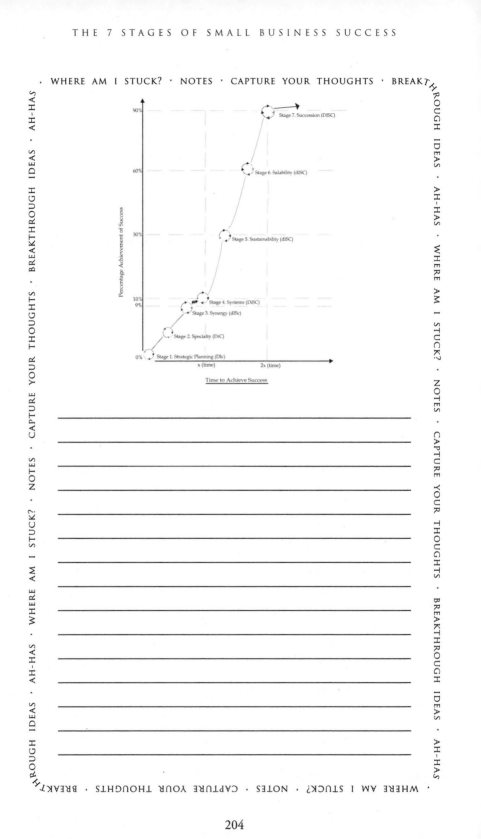

strong direction, robust sales, consistent systems, and high quality. You've created a culture of I³Q. You now get to reap the rewards of a business created with a legacy in mind.

What can you do with this legacy-type business? You can pass it along to another generation. You can donate the business. You can bequeath that business to somebody else. You can sell it. You can keep it as a cash-producing annuity or asset, by hiring a CEO, so that it supports your causes for future generations.

This leads us to your final hire and fire. You know you are a Stage 7 business, regardless of your exit strategy, the moment you fire yourself from the position of CEO. This means that you hire a CEO and the business runs every bit as well, if not better, in your absence.

LAST THINGS LAST

You've created your exit strategy. You know what's next. Continuing on with your Power Tools, it's time for your succession planning. That will entail going back to your advisory board and leaning on your experts to create or update your will, estate and trusts. This is also the time to start thinking about taxes and asset protection.

You may have decided to get into a new venture: spin off a division, create a new product, or take up the hobby. Then you take your venture, product, division or enterprise and begin the Success Cycle at Stage 1 again.

You are about to go where very few have gone. You've gone all the way through the Success Cycle to Stage 7, and you can continue in three-year rotations to build out the products, divisions, ideas, hobbies and

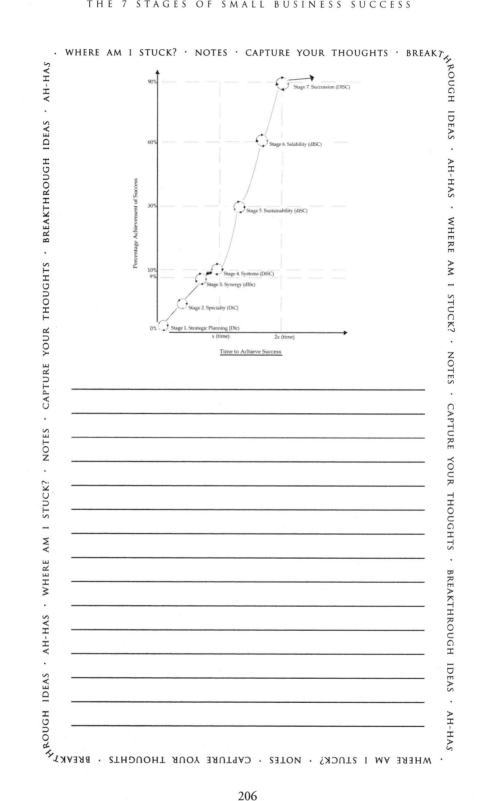

whims. You can do it in such a way that you achieve your vision, going from startup to seven figures in three years or less.

Congratulations, you have just navigated *The 7 Stages of Small Business Success*. You've gone from startup to seven figures in three years or less, and you've learned a lot along the way. You've planned your dream. You've created the structure. You've built the systems. You I³Qed across the board. You left a legacy of talent, a valuable brand, and a unique image. You created lasting value well beyond your years. You've protected your assets. Most important, once you moved forward, you decided what was next for you.

I congratulate you on what you have achieved. Now that you've done it once, you can do it again. Once you have navigated the 7 stages of your success, you will be on to your next DISCoverY.

Tree**Neutral**